T0170897

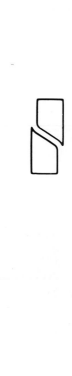

 *Shawnee Books*

Also in this series

*The New Madrid Earthquake: A Midwesterner's
Survival Guide*
William Atkinson

*Foothold on a Hillside: Memories of a
Southern Illinoisan*
Charless Caraway

A Nickel's Worth of Skim Milk
Robert J. Hastings

A Penny's Worth of Minced Ham
Robert J. Hastings

FISHING
SOUTHERN ILLINOIS

Art Reid

Southern Illinois University Press

Carbondale and Edwardsville

Printed in the United States of America
Designed by Loretta Vincent
Production supervised by Natalia Nadraga
89 88 87 86   4 3 2 1

Library of Congress Cataloging-in-Publication Data
Reid, Art, 1926–
   Fishing southern Illinois.
   1. Fishing—Illinois.   I. Title.
SH489.R45   1986   799.1'773   86-3717
ISBN 0-8093-1294-8
ISBN 0-8093-1295-6 (pbk.)

This book is for all fishermen in Southern Illinois who provided the author with the never-ending pleasure of their association; and for my children: Steven, Michael, Matthew, John, Lorna, Melba Marie, and Rebecca. It is especially for my wife, Melba.

Contents

Illustrations

Following Page 80

Preface

SOUTHERN ILLINOIS IS a rare geographical region, rich in fishing opportunities and fishing history. Few locales across the nation have so much to offer so many. Central and much of Northern Illinois are level, vast, with oceans of corn and soybean fields unbroken by trees. Then, to the south, an entirely different Illinois emerges with a complexity of hills and forest, streams and lakes with undeniably good fishing. In fact, some of the best fishing in the state, perhaps the Midwest, begins and ends right here in Southern Illinois.

It could be argued that a few northern states have more fishing waters within similar geographical expanses. This is true, particularly of Minnesota and Wisconsin, to cite just two examples, though they do not offer the tremendous variety of fish species found in the average Southern Illinois lake. Nor do all fishing waters or states offer the generous array of facilities commonplace to public waters in Illinois.

This writer has been fortunate to travel widely over North America. We have also fished a few of the world's renowned places from Alaska to Australia, Mexico, Cuba, Central American nations, and more. The facilities taken for granted by Illinois anglers would be the grandest luxury imaginable in many of these places.

But, of course, I'm talking about the untamed jungles or the pristine woods of Canada. To the contrary, there is more concrete in the combined launching ramps of Rend Lake and Lake Shelbyville in Southern Illinois than can be found over a 200-mile stretch of the Columbia River. During the time it takes the average bass fisherman in Eastern Washington to reach productive water, his Southern Illinois counterpart would have fished for hours, returned home, cleaned the fish, and have had time to cook and eat them should he choose to do this.

There is a large variety of fish in Southern Illinois—from the ever-popular bluegill to tiger muskies, from largemouth black bass to walleye and striped bass, crappie, catfish, white bass and northern pike, and many more. These are fish that a lot of nonresidents travel a long way and spend big bucks to catch. A five-pound bass is a common size in this region. This is a weight that the average fisherman nationwide would gladly trade his tickets to the Super Bowl to catch.

That's what this book is all about—the fish and where they are found in Southern Illinois, the fishermen who have caught them, those who still do, and those who have a burning desire to know more about this most popular of all participation sports.

There is a great deal of fascinating history involved here—not only about fishing and tackle through the ages to that presently used, but more recent history about people, fishermen, places, and events in Southern Illinois. Perhaps what many of us who were around 25 to 30 years ago tend to overlook is that younger generations may not have heard of people such as the late Bill Harkins, of Carterville; Jim Aaron and Bill McCabe or Paul Barnwell, all of Marion; Al Peithman, of Carbondale; John Swetz, of Royalton; Don Gentry, Haskell "Hack" Jackson, Fred Washburn, Jesse Farmer, and scores of other expert anglers. The substantial contributions of these men, and others, to the evolution of contemporary fishing methods and notable events are documented here.

Southern Illinois indeed is traditionally rich in fishing history and I was fortunate enough to be a participant in a small segment of it. For this reason, it is much easier for me (and substantially more factual for you) to call habitually on personal reflections instead of relying on hearsay alone.

Those whom I hesitantly call the "old timers" will understand and appreciate that Bill Harkins and Al Peithman were my fishing mentors, good friends, and faithful counselors. They had patience with a relatively ignorant newcomer to Southern Illinois, and both men will figure prominently throughout this book.

If there is one other person to whom this author feels overwhelming gratitude it is John Gardner, who was quick to recognize that fishing and fishermen of Southern Illinois should receive deserved, conspicuous attention in the *Southern Illinoisan* newspaper. And he selected me to do that. Obviously, I thought that Gardner was gifted with especially good taste.

The reader should be forewarned that, because largemouth black bass is the most popular species in Southern Illinois, a great deal of time and space will be spent examining this species. This does not mean that other popular fish will be shortchanged. Whether you are a card-carrying member of the bluegill club, or whatever species may be your favorite, all will be thoroughly covered.

There is no special effort to list or discuss the various species in order of their respective popularities. Frankly, I don't know whether more people fish for bluegill than for crappie, channel catfish, or whatever. I'm not sure that anyone else knows this for sure.

One of the questions often asked of this writer is what is his favorite species. Risking an uproar among bass fishermen, my favorite is not necessarily the largemouth black bass. To the contrary, I can get just as worked up over catching a 12-ounce bluegill, which is large for this species, as I do boating a larger than average crappie, a five-pound channel cat, or an ugly-faced little bullhead. My favorite, then, is the species I happen to be fishing for at the time.

It has been my experience that power, verve, and speed incorporated in a respectable size channel cat beats hands down the same size largemouth bass. This opinion is based on a number of occasions unparalleled with excitement and thrills that will be recounted in these chapters. For that matter, a 10-pound steelhead can run out 100 yards of fishing line before a channel catfish of the same size can stumble out of the starting blocks. So all things and all fish are relative. Perhaps in relation to each other, ounce for ounce, a bluegill is stronger than a bass. But no one really knows whether or not this is a fair comparison. Nevertheless, these and many other questions will be explored and discussed in this volume.

It is impossible for me to give credit here to everyone who has helped me over the years. Through the years everyone—from all those in the Illinois Department of Conservation (DOC) to the wide-eyed little kids on the shorelines—has been especially cooperative.

It will become apparent to the reader that a great deal of the technical data included here was provided by the Illinois DOC, specifically from its office in Benton. Without this extremely important information to bolster my own records, to update the data concerning the largest fish of various species caught in Illinois, much which is included here would not have been as thorough.

The old saying that some of us can't see the trees for the forest also applies here. Standing too close to the picture often obscures its intricate detail, which I'm guilty of in relation to Southern Illinois University at Carbondale. Its Zoology Department staff members, in particular, have contributed immensely to the fishing scene of Southern Illinois. Without their dedication to research and implementation it is unlikely that fish and fishing in this region would be nearly as advanced as they are.

Now, let's find out where those fish are and how to catch a few.

FISHING SOUTHERN ILLINOIS

1.

Techniques, Lure Presentations, Weather

Techniques

More fish of all species are caught under very weak light conditions than during the brightest daylight hours. Of these weak light conditions early morning prior to and an hour or so following sunup is by far the most productive time. The eyes of many fish species are not adapted to function at peak capacity in strong light. They do not have eyelids to shield from light or take it in, nor do the eyes of fish dilate to perform the same function. In order to regulate the amount of light acceptable to them, then, fish either go up or down, using the water depth to find a compatible light condition. For this reason alone, usually, the clearer the water the deeper fish will be found during bright sunny hours.

Research conclusively shows there is a marked difference between feeding activities of fish, especially bass, in early morning and late evening into the night hours. The odds are heavily stacked in favor of morning. This activity slows soon after sunrise; there is least activity during midday, then perhaps some again about sundown, though it does not equal that of predawn and sunup.

If bass are successful in taking food at dawn there is no reason for them to forage again the same day. In late spring and summer when the digestive systems of these fish work at full speed it takes approximately 48 hours for them to process the contents of a full stomach. Obviously, not all bass everywhere even in the same lake prowl for food at the same time. Of those out searching not all are successful.

We can assume it is these fish with gnawing hunger pains that try again later the same day, perhaps in late evening. If conditions are right they may also try to find food throughout the day! And it's these times which help to fill fishing with so much challenge. Just when you think you have bass all figured out they do the unexpected.

Overcast days with solid cloud mass block enough sunlight to help bass see reasonably well, so on these days, generally, this species is active for a longer time. It's not uncommon to catch bass at midmorning, noon, or if the overcast persists they may feed off and on all day. In this respect we won't single out bass as the only species that may react this way to darkened sky. The eyes of all fish species in Southern Illinois are structured approximately the same. A ceiling of clouds often provides the dimness for all fish to remain in relatively shallow water looking for food.

It was on one of these days when my son, Steve, and I caught the largest bass, a five pounder, about 2:00 P.M., a time when ordinarily a stick of dynamite wouldn't float up a bass that size. We had been on Little Grassy Lake since dawn, and found ruefully little to brag about until the first bass was caught about 8:30 that morning. As this one barely made two pounds it didn't look promising. Conditions weren't at all encouraging because a smacking breeze from the southwest made it difficult to hold the boat in position, and I was mulling over suggesting that we opt for ham and eggs.

We had been fishing with plastic worms sunk to the bars and points, and the stout wind put great curving bows in our lines, flapping them around out of control. Then Steve suggested that we forget this non-sense and troll back toward the boat launching ramp at the north end of the lake near the dam. This was a fine idea, taking me closer, quicker, to those ham and eggs, maybe a couple of pancakes too, and at the moment hashbrowns didn't sound too bad either. We then substituted Bombers for plastic worms.

The Bombers prowled and bounced over the lake bottom running perhaps 10 feet deep; above us the steely overcast remained solid. Suddenly, Steve yipped that he had a fish, and just as suddenly the thought of breakfast vanished. Steve's bass weighed nearly four pounds, the first of four we would catch this dull day from about 9:30 A.M. to 3:00 P.M. The reason we quit the lake when we did was that all cloud cover had disappeared.

Partially overcast days may produce the same results, when fish take advantage of sporadic low-light intensity to visit feeding stations. Generally, though, there will be fewer bass evident than there will be other, more gregarious species.

While some fish species such as bluegill and crappie run in large schools, bass generally are found in groups, especially following the spawn and throughout the rest of the year. And what these bass groups do when they go on the prowl for food is to come up from their sanctuaries to relatively shallow water, then spread out, possibly to minimize competition. Here, they go to known objects of structure—stumps, brush, or whatever—where they can seclude themselves while waiting in ambush for forage.

There is a definite pattern to the size of bass caught with the first cast or two of the morning. You can absolutely rely on it; the first fish will be the largest of a particular spot.

The pecking order of bass is no different than it is in all wildlife and with domestic animals and birds. There is a dominant animal, bird, or fish in every group. And this is the undisputed boss, taking first choice of everything. This pattern is the same from Southern Illinois to Florida, through Mexico to Cuba, Central America, or wherever bass are found. Thus the first fish or two caught from any given hole will be the largest. So, when you bend that bass rod with the initial cast of the morning, brace yourself.

This same awareness of the pecking order also tells us a great deal more about the spot we are fishing. For example, if the first fish or two is undesirably small, then we are casting in the wrong place in order to catch large bass. It also holds true that if the first bass or two caught from an individual spot weighs, say, about three pounds, others here will be this same size or less. It is rare, however, to catch more than three bass in rapid succession from one spot or group, no matter how many fish may be using this place.

I'm convinced that most fish species have an alarm system triggered by being stressed, in this case being hooked by fishermen. This appears to be especially true under normal fishing conditions for average lakes with average fish populations. When this alarm goes off other nearby fish respond by either leaving or remaining dormant until their habitat settles down again, the danger passed.

This does not apply to lakes with abnormal fish populations such as relatively new lakes heavily stocked in Mexico or in the United States. In these places young bass swarm like honeybees. Competition among them for food is especially fierce, so it's not uncommon to catch a dozen or more with repeated cast to the same spot. As lakes age these tremendous populations of uniform-size fish decrease, giving way to established populations of bass in the various age and size groups. Southern Illinois lakes are in this category.

When two or three bass are quickly boated and the action stops, chances are the rest of the fish in the immediate grouping were spooked to deeper water. When this happens your options are limited; you can risk leaving to try another spot, returning later, or stay right there and wait, hoping for fish to return.

There is no guarantee, of course, that either tactic will pay off. Sometimes fish are in a catchable posture for minutes, other times for an hour or more. Your decision may also hinge on how much competition you have from other fishermen looking for a spot to drop anchor and settle in with infinite patience. An impressive number of tournaments have been won by fishermen who opted to hang in there and wait out the fish.

Notable among such tournaments was one on Little Grassy Lake when Mattoon angler, Patrick Kress, who was boated with Jim Aaron, of Marion, won the contest by using only a thimbleful of gas. For two full tournament days Kress and Aaron anchored the boat and fished a single deep hole. Kress caught just one bass each day and took all the marbles and chalk. Each bass topped six pounds!

It is also typical of a particular spot at a particular depth of water to yield bass of a uniform weight. Large bass stay deep, especially during daylight hours. In the average lake it is rare to find six pounder or better trophy fish in water less than eight to ten feet deep throughout the summer or winter. It is not uncommon, however, during spawning season to catch this size bass near shoreline waters.

An excellent example of how some bass can be spooked, although with a little time they return and stay within casting reach, was demonstrated on Barkley Lake, Kentucky. When this lake was just a few years old many Southern Illinoisans fished it regularly, nearly every summer weekend.

One morning, John "Gino" Swetz and I found the mother lode of three-pound bass frequenting an insignificant little point or bar, loaded with brushy stickups. The only feature of this submerged structure, setting it apart from many others like it, was the exceptionally steep drop-off to very deep water. It was a place made for bass to be stacked like cordwood, and they were.

It took only a half dozen casts of spinner baits slithering four to five feet deep through brush to reduce the bass population by three. Then, bass suddenly disappeared. It was as though we had caught them all; that small world of bassdom was now in our boat. So why hang around? Let's go find another willing group, and we did. An hour or so later, however, we swung the boat back to that little point and quickly snatched up two or three more bass, all from about the same four- to five-foot depth, and with the same lures.

Now we were curious about where those spooked bass were going, how far, how deep, so we changed tactics by probing deeper water with plastic worms. The first cast of a weighted plastic worm located bass about 12 feet down. Swetz and I did no more scurrying around from spot to spot. We stayed right there and eventually caught our limit.

There are also times when, for no apparent reason and at what seems like an odd time of day, bass suddenly leave deep holes and migrate upward. This can occur when the sun is so bright it makes your eyelids nervous. Generally, bass in warm summer water move into areas with food at least once each day. This invasion is routinely carried out during weak light. But, now it hasn't and the curious wonder why it hasn't. Under these circumstances, if you have the time to spare, don't be hasty in leaving the lake. Bass may suddenly move up from deep water when you least expect them to. Obviously, this is not a certainty. But when the sun is highest and your eyelids are squinted to half-mast blocking out intense glare, you might begin to catch fish.

One reason largemouth black bass hold so much fascination for so many people is because they are so unpredictable. A reliable trait, however, is that bass definitely will hit a lure out of pure instinctive cussedness as well as from hunger. In fact, if we had to rely on catching only those bass savagely jumping into watery supermarkets it would not be worth the bother to fish for them.

We catch most bass because they are opportunistic predators by nature, and not because they are particularly hungry. In all of nature hunger is an ongoing condition, never ceasing, always there uppermost in the minds of the predator be it animal, bird, or fish. Predators kill to survive, and they are very good at what they do. In the case of fishermen, the artificial lures used are the would-be victims of bass. Put the right lure at the right time near enough to a bass and it's a hooked fish, triggered to action by the predator's instinct to not let an opportunity pass. There are few bass fishermen with a few years of lake water boiling up behind their outboard motors, who have not caught bass loaded to the gullets with food. These fish have taken so much natural food, such as gizzard shad, threadfin shad, etc., that we marvel, wondering why they could possibly be interested in a lure.

It is humanly impossible to crank the handle of a fishing reel so fast that a bass cannot grab the lure. Summer bass are very swift. They move faster than a person going to the bank to cash a large check. Bass and other fish species take lures only because they believe them to be natural forage, and the reality of this matter is that most food they eat daily is almost, but not quite, as swift as they are. Picking off the weak and disabled of the minnow family is easy for a bass to do. Even these small fish swim faster than most lures travel, so catching a crankbait, buzzbait, or plastic worm is easy.

Most of the time bass are not great sprinters after food. They don't chase helter-skelter. They wait until something edible comes near. This is why so many times we make repeated casts to an area without results, then suddenly get a hit when the lure passes through what we think is the same route it took a couple times before. Perhaps it didn't. More likely the lure was going just a little wide of this fish's particular chase zone. This is also why saturation casting of all water results in catching the most bass. There are times when you can pound water to a bubbling froth without getting a nod of recognition, then finally catch a bass which was there all the time.

One day Bill Harkins and I caught a four-pound bass on the fourteenth cast of a Lunker Lure. It was spring on Crab Orchard Lake, bass were near shorelines and as they often are this one was offended by the noisy lure, though his jab at it was only a warning. As it was Harkins' buzzbait which had located the fish, and this obviously was a one-on-one situation, my subordinate role in the episode was that of human calculator as Harkins made casts. I started counting. Each time the lure landed with pinpoint accuracy and came back over the exact spot where the bass had roiled up under it. When I reached a count of a dozen unanswered flings, I was ready to move on when Harkins optimistically said, "Just one more cast." He lied a little by making two, of which the second indeed was the last. The hooked bass jumped half the distance to the boat.

In summer water bass do the same. For whatever reason, they migrate up from deep water, spread out among the stumps, brush, or rocks and just rest doing nothing at all. Oftentimes bass hover at various depths between bottom and surface while these do-nothing postures generally are among fragments of brush and other solid objects as though the fish desperately need something to lean against. Importantly, these fish don't move more than a foot or so to suck in the most delicious food in the lake. So, lures must be presented repetitiously until it becomes impossible for the opportunistic instinct of the predator to ignore.

Lure Presentations

Actively feeding fish are the easiest of all to catch. You heave, you crank, and you hope the lure covers the right path. Many times it does because fish are in a chasing mood. Under these circumstances the lure can't be run fast enough. Now, we catch bass because they don't want to let any possible chunk of food slip past them. They spin around and pounce.

I'm certain that the lure itself is relatively insignificant. Whether it is the latest highly touted crank bait or a beer can tab makes no real difference to bass. In fact, while at Lake Guerrero in Mexico, I was happy to become an indispensable partner in an experiment with a beer can tab rigged with hooks. I volunteered to provide a sufficient number of empty cans.

At that time, Ed Houer, who made the lures, was producer/director of our TV series, and he was filming the action. For him, lures made from beer can tabs were not that great a challenge. We caught just as many, if not more, bass on Hauer's artificials as we did with conventional lures. Not surprisingly, the brand of beer was not a factor. Bass indiscriminately gulped tabs of various brands. Bass not engaged in frenetic feeding activity become far greater challenges for all the Ed Houers of the fishing world. Importantly, we try to catch nonfeeding bass more often than we are fortunate enough to find them scooting here and there slashing at everything thrown their way.

First, let's separate the lures into categories. For this exercise we'll call crank baits exactly that. These are lures which are designed to perform best with steady high-speed retrieves. Some in this category go deeper than others. Some, when they are idle, float to the surface while others sink. But for now we won't be concerned about any crank bait characteristics other than performance when drawn through the water. All these baits have two things in common; they have solid bodies and they resemble some species of natural forage for bass. In recent years the typical crank bait has been meticulously painted to resemble closely the prey species.

Spinner baits are an entirely different lure and category. The typical spinner bait has either one or two metal blades which revolve or spin, hence the name. Compared with crank baits, spinner lures are equally or even more versatile as they can be fished from the surface to any depth.

Finally there are the weighted plastic worms and jigs and eels, which latter are also called "jig and pig" with pork rind on the hook. These come under the same heading because they are simply variations of each other, and they are manipulated the same way.

When you are using crank baits in water you believe holds fish, change your speed of retrieve, experiment with various speeds until you find the one compelling to the fish. It occasionally also pays off to run the crank bait as fast as possible, then suddenly stop, hesitate for a second or two before resuming cranking.

The importance of finding the right speed is never more evident than when trolling. You chug along in more or less a straight line, then swing the boat around to the opposite direction. While in this turn, the lure changes speed, slows, falls a little deeper and is struck by a fish. The pattern to repeat, then, is fish a little deeper and impart an occasional halting action to the lure.

There are days when bass take spinner baits retrieved steadily, and there are other days when this method won't buy a strike. Here again, try the change-up. Cast the lure and let it sink to bottom, then activate it by sharply raising the rod tip. Now, stop and allow the spinner bait to fall back, flutter, while you take up slack line. Bass often want to see these lures wafting down to them, right in front of their big mouths, so they inhale them on the descent.

This is the same procedure successfully used with plastic worms and jigs and eels, and even with spinner baits with plastic worms or pork strips on their hooks. It is that up and down, steady but slow, hesitant manipulation of these lures which entices reluctant fish to strike.

It is not only possible but likely to fish plastic worms too slowly. Remember that a bass' food is elusive, capable of high-speed escape. A creepy crawly plastic worm is a nothing speed for bass to overtake. And if this lures fails to motivate the impulsive predatory instinct it will be ignored. There is an old saying about plastic worm fishing: "Don't let the lure sit on the bottom." To the contrary, keep it moving up and down on and off the bottom by using the same rod-stroking action mentioned earlier with spinner baits.

Generally, the secret to catching summer bass with any artificial lure is intricately connected with the floor of the lake. No matter what depth bass happen to be on a particular day, they will be snuggled closely to the bottom. The exception would be when they hover, and it is most difficult to determine at which depth they are hovering. When this happens bass are found among something tangible such as limbs of trees standing in the water, or very tall weeds. They can be located by fishing straight down with lures jigged and bounced at all depths.

This is as good a time as any to mention that although the bulk of the foregoing specifically singles out the bass species, the same places, methods, and techniques also apply to catching most fish species in Southern Illinois. The only notable difference would be the size of lures used. Obviously, the smaller the fish the smaller the lure, and vice versa.

For example, crappie take small spinner baits and jigs just as quickly as bass take larger sizes, and bluegill do the same to still smaller lures of this type. If walleye are present you are just as likely to hook them as you are bass on any of the above-mentioned artificials. Stripers (rock fish) and white bass are equally fooled by lures of the appropriate size. Even catfish occasionally attack artificials, and a friend of mine became the most surprised bass fisherman in the nation the time he hooked and landed a 20-pound carp that struck his plastic worm. Most kinds of fish are attracted by underwater structure similar to those described here. In the average lake this desirable habitat is at a premium, so fish of many species gather to use it. This is also a matter of survival for all species. In the underwater food chain the large eat the small, etc., down the line until the smallest feed on aquatic vegetation, algae, or plankton suspended in the water.

Weather

In one way or another all creatures are affected by weather. Some of these changes are subtle while others are pronounced. Although I'm not convinced that anyone knows beyond a shadow of a doubt what makes fish behave the way they do under certain weather conditions, we do know how some of them respond to some patterns. The most predictable of all fish responses and the weather change they respond to is what they do following a severe cold front. They do virtually nothing. So this is the worst possible time to go fishing.

A cold front is any mass of dry chilly air moving into a region to replace a mass of hot, humid air. Generally, this adversely affects fishing results. It is very important to remember that the adversity does not become evident until the cold front dominates the regional weather, until after the warm air mass has been shoved out. Then, clear skies prevail, and fishing efforts flunk the acid test.

In this day of enlightment and scuba diving gear we know where fish are under these conditions because they are seen in the depths. Yet what particular element or combination of weather factors put them there is anyone's guess. Perhaps, as many people believe, they hole up in dark corners to escape the light brilliance of cloudless days during the aftermath of these fronts.

The typical cold front works this way and changes things: First, there is normal seasonal weather. It is warm to hot and humid. The breeze, if any at all, is from the prevailing southwest direction, and there have been clouds. During this time fishing results have been fair to good because, again, this is the normal Southern Illinois summer weather.

Now, a cold front approaches. Ahead of it are ominous clouds, perhaps dark and forbidding and loaded with moisture. This is a massive front which overwhelms everything in its path and settles in. But this front, too, is only temporary. Southern Illinois weather is noted for being unreliable, so according to pattern the front leaves in its wake a clear blue sky. Fishing goes downhill in a hand basket, and it will be days before it improves.

Returning to normality is entirely dependent upon the severity of the cold front. Some are more powerful than others. Many fronts bound through a region and are gone before anyone really notices them, particularly when it's 95 degrees with humidity to match, but nothing seems to change. The mildest of fronts trigger only slight reactions in fish while the strongest, more drastic changes spoil fishing for a few days.

What we have is not what we think we should have. Now, the weather is delightful, cool and pleasant, invigorating enough to stimulate a full day on the lake. But we don't catch fish. And we won't catch many at all until weather conditions revert to their normal pattern for the season. This turnabout includes winds from the south or southwest bringing warm, humid air and more clouds, even though high and thin, than have been around for a few days. As long as this condition hangs in there fishing results will be normal.

In direct contrast to the skimpy results of fishing following a cold front is what might happen just before this front arrives, and as the slate-gray sky blocks the sun. Generally, fish are very active. Coming in on the smacking breeze to fish summer holes could be the best hours spent all season. You have a good chance of catching fish the full day, anytime of day. If this happens to be a slow-moving front lasting a day or more, fish might stay active while this weather prevails.

Calling on years of scribbled records jotted down while in boats all over Southern Illinois, I come up with a clear pattern of what worked for companions and me at the time. Some of the most sensational fish production periods were those times prior to and during drastic weather changes such as just described. The funkiest days on lakes were those on the heels of these fronts. The most reliable fishing weather consists of hot, humid, still days.

Yet another excellent time to be fishing is just before and following local unsettled weather which does not completely displace or interfere with the prevailing regional weather condition. Generally, this takes the form of local thunderstorms. If anything, it is hotter and more humid after these storms pass. Obviously, if there is lightning in these storms you don't want to become a lightning rod and get yourself sizzled. People in boats make high-profile targets on flat water. No fish is worth getting scorched for, but keep in mind that when it is safe again to venture back out, this could be an excellent move.

Fishing during spring weather conditions is an entirely different matter. Then, too, fish are motivated by different instincts than they are in summer. It appears that in spring most fish species are more or less automatically drawn by instinct to comparitively shallow water, which happens to be the warmest, in preparation for spawning. Here, the water temperature is compatible with spawning because of bright sunshine on clear days.

It is also in spring following these clear days when late afternoons and evenings often produce the best results for shoreline fishing. Then, let the typical seasonal cold front come banging in resoundingly to upset this serenity and no amount of darkening cloud cover will keep fish in these shallows. They disappear.

Just before fish spawn, bright sunny days often produce the better fishing. Following the reproduction period, however, fish revert to normal behavior in conjunction with summer water temperatures and brilliant days as opposed to those with cloud cover and their reaction to severe changes such as cold fronts.

There is also a very brief span of time in spring when on any given especially hot, sticky day shallow hovering bass, in particular, will provide stunning performances. These are male bass with all the earmarks of cabin fever. They are irritable, very hungry, and anxious to separate themselves from parental responsibility. These are bass that have spent days guarding eggs in nests, then the fry. When it comes time to abandon this project they often do it scornfully, leaving fry to fend for themselves. If a fisherman just happens to be near throwing lures these bass also have the decency to hit artificials in a manner we seldom experience.

Kermit Keim, of Murphysboro, and I were fortunate to share one of these unusual occurrences. It was the first time we fished together. It was May, so humid that to sit cross-legged would leave our legs stuck together like Band-Aids, and Keim and I were to meet at noon. Frankly, I didn't hold much hope for any success bass fishing because the fish had been inactive while spawning.

When I arrived at the dock an hour ahead of Keim, it was 85 degrees and climbing, without a cloud in the sky, so I decided at least to make a preliminary investigation of a nearby cove before breaking the sad news to my companion not to expect much action. Inside that cove the whole lake seemed to be alive with bass—tormented, infuriated bass that tried to rip the surface lures to shreds. These were the same fish, the same spawning bass, that had on different occasions revealed themselves to this writer casting this same stretch of shoreline. Then, however, they had tried to stun the lure, drive it away. Nothing more.

Now, within minutes, there were three bass in the boat. From combined heat, humidity, and a high state of excitement I was drenched with sweat. Struggling with the anxiety of wanting to continue to fish this rare moment, but with some guilt for having done so, I relented and dashed back to the dock hoping that Keim was there waiting. He jumped in the boat and we returned to the cove to clash with more bass.

Three more bass delivered hammering blows to our lures. Two of them were especially ferocious, and one in particular caused more than its rightful share of problems. In rushing into the boat and being forced to rig up his casting gear during the fever-racked dash back to this cove, Keim was not given the opportunity to secure the reel to the rod as it should have been. When he set the hook on this fish the reel separated from the rod! He looked at it with an expression of surprise. He grabbed the line, dropping both rod and reel, and hand-over-hand snatched it in with unimaginable quickness. The bass flopped in the boat.

This fish, like each of the others, weighed between three and four pounds. We were pleasantly satiated with the results. And that day was regarded as something of a classic. The day was hot and nasty humid, a clear sky and high noon, when these fish went on a rampage, consumed with desire to hit something.

Perhaps that was one of the best examples of unpredictability in this whole fishing business. We don't know from day to day how fish will respond. Weather being what it is and fish being what they are, conditions and responses to them often change by the hour, so it is impossible to predict fishing conditions very far in advance.

2.

Lakes and Rivers

IT IS DIFFICULT to define the boundaries of Southern Illinois. People who live in Cairo obviously find no problem with the definition, while residents of Mattoon or Jacksonville might consider themselves more central than southern. In order to establish fairly waterfowl hunting seasons throughout this 400-mile-long state, the Illinois Department of Conservation uses three zones—northern, central, and southern. The southern zone includes all lands below Route 50. This discussion does not deal with waterfowl hunting, however, so if we cling to this same boundary an immense amount of fishing water would be excluded.

So, let's define Southern Illinois geographically, beginning where the land itself changes from flat fields of black farmland where trees are oddities to undulating hills covered with brushy forests. This region, then, would also include Lake Shelbyville and fishing waters within a range directly east and west of that point. This is not to say, however, that every small lake, large pond, or creek will be covered in this text. We will concentrate our efforts on waters that receive the lion's share of attention from anglers, plus a few that do not but should receive more notice.

Nor will the author try to document seasons, fishing license fees, catch limits of various species, or regulations imposed on certain waters that do not apply statewide. Most of this is common knowledge, or at least it should be for the individuals who plan to use fishing facilities. Much of this information is as close as your nearest sporting goods store, or you can contact the Benton office of the Illinois Department of Conservation, RR 4, Box 68, Benton, Illinois 62812. Phone (618) 435-8138. Rules, regulations, and catch limits are ever-changing. For examples, there are minimum size limits on large-mouth black bass in certain lakes, which set these lakes apart from others. So, the specific rules for individual waters should be familiar to the angler.

Public lakes will be listed in alphabetical order, which places Lake Baldwin first. The size of each body of water, its location, and fish species it contains will be of paramount consideration here.

Lake Baldwin

Lake Baldwin is a 2,200-acre warm-water reservoir north of Baldwin in Randolph County. This is an Illinois Power Company lake opened to the public in 1971 in cooperation with the Illinois Department of Conservation. From its early days it has been an outstanding lake for bass and crappie, though in recent years bass fishing production has leveled off. Baldwin also has channel catfish and flatheads, bluegill, white bass, and introduced striped bass. These are hybrid stripers which generally average more than four pounds. Baldwin is one of the lakes that has special rules and fishing hours.

Carlyle Lake

Carlyle, with nearly 25,000 surface acres, is the largest reservoir in the state. It straddles sections of three counties—Clinton, Fayette, and Bond. The city of Carlyle is at the southern tip of the lake. It is almost dead center between four major highways, Routes 70, 50, 51, and 127.

This huge impoundment was created by damming the Kaskaskia River, so perhaps it's not surprising that some fish species common to Illinois rivers, such as drum, are found in Carlyle. This water has everything else too, including largemouth bass, crappie, bluegill, channel cats and bullheads, white bass and walleye. Flathead catfish grow big and powerful in Carlyle, making this species the largest in the lake. The average weight of flathead caught is around 25 pounds.

Completed in 1966, Lake Carlyle has an 85-mile shoreline. It covers about 15 miles in length and about 3 miles in width. But it's a shallow lake averaging only 11 feet, which also makes it a rough body of water under windy conditions. This shallowness also creates a fishing problem in the hottest summer weeks. In a shallow lake, below 12 feet or so there is little dissolved oxygen to sustain fish life. The angler won't want to waste time and effort probing deeper for fish. The northern one-third of the lake is perhaps best for all-around fishing potential, particularly for the sunfish family and catfish.

Cedar Lake

Owned by the city of Carbondale and jointly managed by the U.S. Forest Service, Cedar Lake was built for a water reservoir, and the by-product is fishing. It has two main access roads, off Route 51 about 6 miles south of Carbondale and east off Route 127 some 10 miles south of Murphysboro. With 1,750 acres, Cedar Lake is without question the largest of the midsize lakes this author has ever fished. It is long and slim and filled with bluegill, crappie, redear sunfish, both large-mouth and spotted bass, channel catfish, and walleye. This has proved to be one of the better walleye waters in Southern Illinois. Cedar has all the appearances of a lake where one can catch bass, and in this case the angler is not mislead. This species will average 2 pounds or more. But, as with Lake Baldwin, facilities here are limited to nonexistent, though there are excellent launching ramps and parking lots.

Crab Orchard Lake

This is one of the oldest lakes in this region. Built in 1940, it has 7,000 acres reaching more than eight miles between Marion and Carbondale. A portion of Crab Orchard is on the north side of Route 13. This is one of three lakes within the jurisdiction of the Crab Orchard National Wildlife Refuge. Crab Orchard indeed has served Southern Illinois well. There was a time when it was regarded as having the finest bass fishing in the area if not in the state. Also, it was and still is a tremendous fishery for channel catfish.

This lake has been a proving ground for a number of experimental fish introductions by both the U.S. Fish and Wildlife Service and Southern Illinois University at Carbondale. Notable among them are stocked striped bass, walleye, and threadfin shad. The best of the three was the threadfin, which enhanced this lake's game species populations.

Crab Orchard is considered a shallow body of water with an average depth not exceeding 8 feet, though there are spots ranging to 25 and 30 feet deep. Like Carlyle Lake and many others in Southern Illinois, Crab Orchard stratifies in the hottest weather, so oxygen is skimpy at best below 10 feet, and then fish become lethargic and extremely difficult to locate.

Despite the stockings of striped bass in this lake, Crab Orchard is not regarded as a good prospect to turn out this trophy fish. There are much better lakes in this region for this species. More prevalent are crappie, bass, bluegill (the only two-pounder of this species ever seen by this writer came from Crab Orchard), channel catfish, drum, carp, white bass, and buffalo fish. It also has an abundance of yellow bass, though few anglers ever try to catch them. Crappie in particular benefited from threadfin shad stocked in Crab Orchard. There are also a few very large catfish (probably flatheads) in this lake.

Devils Kitchen Lake

This is the only lake in Southern Illinois with rainbow trout. These were stocked by the U.S. Fish and Wildlife Service in 1976. DK, as it is called locally, is also within the Crab Orchard National Wildlife Refuge. With its deep, clear water the rainbows have done well in DK. It has slightly more than 800 acres with bass, bluegill, and crappie the main populations. Bluegill are especially fine specimens, and bass have been taken exceeding 10 pounds.

In spring the creek just below the spillway at the dam provides good bullhead fishing. Because of its deep water, summer fish are generally found deeper than in other nearby lakes. The clarity of water also means that during daylight hours fish seek the darkness of the depths.

Devils Kitchen is located about 12 miles south of Carbondale off the Giant City Blacktop Road. This same road runs between the Little Grassy Fish Hatchery and Little Grassy Lake. Approaching from the east, take the Grassy Road off Route 148.

Hillsboro New City Lake

Also called Glenn Shoals Lake, this is one of the newest additions to the fishing waters of Southern Illinois. And a welcome addition it is too, partly because of its striped bass and muskie hybrids. The hybrid muskie is the tiger muskie. Both hybrids have plenty of room in the 1,200-acre impoundment.

Hillsboro New City Lake became a public fishing spot in 1981. Prior to that time, however, it was stocked with fish including bass, bluegill, crappie, and channel catfish plus the striper and muskie hybrids. Hybrid striped bass, or "wipers" as they are often called, are crosses between white bass and stripers. Tiger muskies were created from a mixture of northern pike and muskellunge. Both fish have the capacity to grow big and bold.

The location of this city water reservoir is less than two miles from downtown Hillsboro, just north of the city off Route 127. While this lake remains relatively young, fishing for bass and the other popular species is expected to be better than average.

Horseshoe Lake

Not to be confused with another Horseshoe Lake in the north, this always will be the epitome of excellent panfishing in Southern Illinois. Horseshoe Lake is as deep south as one can get in this state. This writer has claimed for years that we could take anyone from central Illinois north to Chicago, suddenly plunk them down in the middle of the night at Horseshoe, and at daybreak, Illinois would be their last guess for the state they were really in.

There are lots of bluegill and crappie among those knobby-kneed cypress, tupelo, and gum trees standing in the shallow water. This is a place where one can't see the whole lake for the trees, so Horseshoe gives the appearance of being smaller than its 2,400 acres. It's a very shallow lake, though, averaging less than four feet. Six feet is considered deep for this lake.

Through the years the reputation for bluegill and crappie has nudged aside publicity about bass fishing. Nonetheless, Horseshoe is the only lake to this writer's knowledge that ever gave up a matched pair of nine-pound bass in one day to the same fisherman, and this angler was from Marion.

Horseshoe is in Alexander County just south of Olive Branch off Route 3. It is part of the 8,000-acre wildlife area owned and operated by the Illinois Department of Conservation, the grounds and water being used primarily for wintering Canada geese.

Lake Kincaid

From its opening in 1972, Lake Kincaid has been popular. With 2,750 acres just three miles west of Murphysboro and north of Route 149, this lake gets lots of attention. It is a very good bass lake. It is also good crappie and bluegill water. Kincaid is the only downstate lake to ever bring off a natural spawn of northern pike, which no longer occurs, though many northerns from that batch and from original stocks are in the lake. Also stocked were walleye and striped bass. There are catfish here, too, and a few years ago there were so many small bullheads they were troublesome to bass casters who commonly hooked them by accident with lures.

With an average depth hovering around 18 feet, this is regarded as a deep lake with depths going to about 70 feet. With striped bass, walleye, and northerns mixed with the indigenous species one never knows what one will hook until the fish is seen at the surface. Kincaid, like most regional lakes, is water which at any time is capable of yielding bass to 9 and 10 pounds. And as with most regional lakes, these weights of largemouth bass are not common by any means. Six and seven pounders are more common in Kincaid as elsewhere.

Lake of Egypt

Although E comes before K in the alphabet, L follows K, and because this lake's name is registered as Lake of Egypt it is here placed in its proper slot. Its proper slot in the grand scheme of fishing waters is near to if not leading the list of all bass fishing lakes. Lake of Egypt has 2,300 acres of prime bass water that annually produces so many bass weighing 5 pounds or more they are nearly uncountable.

If there is a lake in Southern Illinois which can be depended upon to give up an impressive though uncommon number of 9-pound bass, this is it. The lake record largemouth bass is 11 pounds 12 ounces! Before the Illinois daily limit of bass was reduced from 10 fish to 6, this writer saw, on a number of occasions, stringers of 10 Lake of Egypt bass which contained total weights of 50 pounds or more.

Water averages about 18 feet deep with a maximum depth of about 50 feet, and within it are also excellent weights of crappie and bluegill. Lake of Egypt is the winter holdover water for threadfin shad, which experiences a complete die-off when water temperatures drop to normal winter temperatures. But here, threadfin survive in the warm water discharge of the Southern Illinois Power Cooperative Plant that built the lake in 1961. So, every fish species in this lake including catfish finds tremendous benefits, grows fast and bulky, from this ever-present food supply. Crappie weighing more than 4 pounds have been caught here. The lake is nine miles south of Marion off Route 37 or east of I-57.

Little Grassy Lake

With 1,000 acres of surface water, Little Grassy is the third and final fishing water within the grounds of the Crab Orchard National Wildlife Refuge. This is also one of the old-timers of the region, and being so it has a widespread reputation for good fishing, particularly for largemouth bass and crappie. A fish of the latter species from Little Grassy held state-record status for many years. The lake record bass topped 10 pounds.

Grassy is another of the dependable lakes to produce bass weighing from 6 to 9 pounds. It is the rare season, in fact, when 9 pounders are not recorded. With an average depth more than 25 feet, Grassy accommodates a good fishery of bluegill and bullhead with some channel catfish, though generally catfishermen do not single out this lake for the deliberate, concentrated efforts they give to other area lakes. The majority of anglers focus attention on bass, bluegill, and crappie. Right next door to Little Grassy is Devils Kitchen Lake, so directions to reach it are the same, though it is about a mile or so closer to Carbondale from Giant City Blacktop Road.

Lou Yaeger

This lake is best known as a crappie fishing lake. Lou Yaeger is near Litchfield in Montgomery County. It is reached by going north on Route 16 or east of I-55. It is a reservoir with more than 1,300 acres. Perhaps Lou Yaeger is like Horseshoe Lake in that crappie get the majority of angler attention while other species get less pressure. Nonetheless, it has ample populations of bass and bluegill, and this is a lot of water to explore for their best hangouts. The lake averages about 10 feet deep with a maximum depth of 40 feet. Yaeger is one of those sleepers, little known outside its immediate area. When aroused by a gentle hand on the throttle it could lead the boated angler to excellent fishing.

Newton Lake

Newton was completely regulated even before it was opened to public fishing. This Jasper County lake about 10 miles from Newton was fully stocked with fish in 1976 and opened four years later. Here, from the outset a bass had to be 18 inches long before it was a legal keeper. The average bass of this length in Newton ranged between 3 and 4 pounds, so there were scads of bass rejected by anglers who would elsewhere cart them home to the skillet. Evidently this measure of conservation has paid off. Walleye stocked at the same time are large, heavy fish. Crappie are stout, and bluegill and channel catfish show an equal amount of growth for these species.

Newton is another warm-water lake created through the auspices of the Central Illinois Public Service Company and given over to the Illinois DOC on a long-term contract to manage the fishery. This lake, like so many others in the whole state of Illinois, came under Illinois Department of Conservation jurisdiction while this government branch was headed by David Kenney, formerly of Carbondale and Southern Illinois University. During his tenure as director of the Illinois Department of Conservation, Kenney did more than any other director to negotiate compatible agreements with power companies covering the length of the state. Without them the fishable water open to the public would be reduced by thousands of acres.

These Newton acres include bass that weigh 10 pounds or more, channel catfish of equal or heavier weights, and crappie that have topped 3 pounds. There is no telling how large the walleye are, though they might make these other species look like minnows. Newton Lake is only 22 miles from Effingham, a center for devoted fishermen, and easily reachable from both I-57 and I-70. Another route to Newton is 130. If you are a trophy hunter, Newton Lake is worth keeping in mind.

Rend Lake

Rend is a 1971 lake that instantly fulfilled the need for fishing water north of Marion, Carterville, Herrin, and Carbondale. In Jefferson and Franklin counties, Rend Lake stretches between Benton and Mt. Vernon on the east and Christopher, Sesser, and Waltonville on the west. Within this vast territory are thousands of anglers who look to Rend to provide the thrills every fisherman hopes to experience. It is a very large body of water, nearly 19,000 acres, 13 miles long, 3 miles wide, and with more than 160 miles of meandering shoreline.

This much water can hold a lot of fish, and it does. White bass, largemouth bass, crappie, bluegill, channel catfish, and flathead make up the complement of species common to Southern Illinois water while the more recently introduced striped bass is the healthy-sized bonus fish. Striped bass are expected to give the flathead a run for honors as the largest species in this lake. Rend also has freshwater drum, yellow bass, and carp.

Bass average a very popular size at nearly 3 pounds, which is a heavy average for the species even in Southern Illinois. This is also a cat-fisherman's lake, particularly for those who jug for channel cats. Semi-truck trailer scales would have to be brought in to weigh the channel catfish taken from Rend any given summer night. If you travel I-57 between Benton and Mt. Vernon you can't miss Rend Lake. It's just about everywhere. Approaches from the west are off Route 148.

Lake Sangchris

This is another fine fishing lake which would not be available to anglers if not for cooperative efforts between its owner, Commonwealth Edison, and the Illinois DOC. Built in 1965 and given state-park status in 1969, Sangchris has 2,165 acres of open water year-round.

In it are bass, channel catfish, bluegill, white bass, and crappie. Bass are rated a shade larger than the average caught in Southern Illinois, and white bass between 1 and 2 pounds hold an especially large average for this species. Though it is not classed as a great bluegill lake, the average size crappie pushing more than 1 pound puts Sangchris in a category of better lakes in the state for this fish.

The lake gets a lot of play from anglers from Taylorville, which city is just eight miles from Sangchris, and from anglers from Springfield, which city is only a fifteen-mile drive away. With nearly a year-round growing season, bass and other species grow fast, so the lake is very popular with bass fishermen and is the site of tournaments.

Lake Shelbyville

Between Champaign and Bondville the Kaskaskia River is small enough for a 10-year-old kid to leap across without getting his sneakers damp. Most people who travel Old Route 10 do not know the Kaskaskia is there. As it courses southward it becomes a full-blown, especially busy river. It worked hard to create massive Carlyle Lake and Baldwin, but before that it stopped off to fill parts of two counties with water called Lake Shelbyville. Shelbyville covers 11,100 acres in Shelby and Moultrie counties. The city of Shelbyville is located on Route 16 at the southwest tip of the lake, Mattoon is directly east of the lake, and Sullivan, at the junction of Routes 32 and 121, is near the northeast corner of the lake. The lake is nearly 20 miles long.

It contains about every fish species known to Illinois and a couple that are relatively new to the state. Bass, crappie, catfish, and white bass, plus bluegill, are the common species. Northern pike, walleye, and muskie are introductions. Shelbyville anglers also occasionally locate smallmouth bass and big flathead catfish in water which averages almost 20 feet deep and has a maximum depth of 67 feet. This is another of many impoundments where fishing below the dam should not be overlooked. There are times when these fast moving tailwaters are far more productive than lake fishing. As a generality, this holds true for impoundments with spillways.

Stephen Forbes Lake

Tucked snugly away near the village of Omega in Marion County, this 525-acre reservoir hasn't made a ripple on the gigantic pool of fisheries in Southern Illinois. Most anglers are not even aware that Stephen Forbes Lake exists.

Yet, for those who are fully aware, this water offers some of the best fishing potential in the region. Bass weighing up to 9 pounds are not uncommon, and hybrid striped bass stocked in 1978 are robust and ready to test those anglers who hook them. Channel catfish get their fair share of attention, too, and bluegill and crappie populations are high.

The lake is not shallow, not deep, but somewhere in between, averaging 14 feet with only 28 feet of water at its deepest. Illinois DOC surveys show that bass in this lake average 2.5 pounds, the average size of hybrid striper is between 2 and 10 pounds, average channel catfish will match the weight of largemouth bass, though bluegill and crappie tend to be smallish. To reach Stephen Forbes Lake from the north the best way is through Kinmundy off I-57, with the lake just four miles east and two miles south. From the opposite direction, turn east on Route 50 at Salem to the road leading north to Omega.

Notes on Other Lakes

Lake Carlinville, at Carlinville, yielded a state-record largemouth black bass that only recently was surpassed by the current state record. The Carlinville Lake fish weighed 12 pounds 8 ounces, which was displaced by a bass topping 13 pounds.

Centralia has a reservoir with excellent bass fishing potential; Lake Charleston near Charleston is noted for channel catfish, bluegill, and crappie; while near McLeansboro is Dolan Lake, where redear sunfish, bluegill, and channel cats are found.

Near Olney is the 935-acre East Fork Lake with all the expected fish species. A fine lake with excellent fishing.

Greenville New City Lake near Greenville now has tiger muskies and hybrid stripers in addition to native species. This 775-acre impoundment is indeed an exciting place to be.

Mermet Lake in Massac County between Routes 45 and 37 is shallow and brushy—a good place to fling surface lures even during the hottest weeks. It has 452 acres of water holding bass, bluegill, crappie, and channel cats.

Though Lake Murphysboro west of Murphysboro in Jackson County has only 146 acres it is one of the best bluegill and redear sunfish waters in Southern Illinois.

Pyramid State Park near Pinckneyville contains 135 acres of very fishable water with bluegill and bass predominating.

Still another larger-than-average reservoir is located at Vandalia. With 660 acres, Vandalia City Lake is well used by area residents who look for catfish, bass, bluegill, and crappie.

Finally, Washington County lake near Nashville is regarded by those who use it regularly as an outstanding fishery for bass, bluegill, crappie, and channel cat. The Illinoise DOC gives this lake very high marks.

Every lake named here is fully capable of providing especially good fishing for a week or lifetime of repeated visitations. The lake with which you are most familiar, whether you spend an occasional day, a week, or fish each day of the month, will be the one where you catch the most fish.

Anglers who are consistently successful pretty much stick to one lake. They might forget some things but they don't forget their best fishing holes. These people can remember every fish of every size landed from every spot as though it all happened five minutes past sunrise this morning. Knowing the water is equated identically with using a particularly favorite artificial lure. You use it because you have confidence in it. The longer it is tied on and the more water it covers, the more fish are fooled by it. Naturally, you think this is the best invention since pockets on shirts, and you would not willingly give it up.

It would be impossible to mention every small lake and city reservoir, all of the strip mine lakes and backwaters off the rivers, in a book of this kind. There are so many of them they indeed would require special emphasis within an entirely separate volume. This has been done, and information of this kind is available from the Illinois Department of Conservation and tourism offices.

Suffice it here to say, then, that the great rivers forming the southern borders of Illinois are the Mississippi and Ohio. Lesser tributaries are the Illinois, Kaskaskia, Wabash, Little Wabash, Big Muddy, and Embarrass. All these waterways offer a variety of fish. Chief among these species are catfish, from channel cats to bullheads, from flatheads to the often monstrous blue cats. The Wabash River, in fact, is noted for the latter catfish species.

As mentioned, excellent fishing often occurs on these rivers below dams and locks, and there are few species included throughout this foregoing list that do not live in these rivers. Those few would be hybrid striped bass, walleye, and tiger muskies, though walleye are in the northern reaches of the Mississippi and Illinois Rivers and in the tail waters below dams on the Kaskaskia. We must remember, too, that the first state-record striped bass (not hybrid) was caught from a backwater off the Ohio River near Mounds. Still, these fish in the largest rivers are not as common as they are in lakes now.

3.

Fish Families and Species

Bass and Sunfish

Largemouth Black Bass.   If bass fishermen had the option to vote for a national symbol, the largemouth black bass (which is a member of the sunfish family) would win by a landslide. In this nation the black bass is unquestionably the one that gives more fishermen more excitement than any other species. One of the many reasons is that black bass are to be found across the nation, accessible to nearly everyone with a cane pole to those who demand the most sophisticated tackle.

Not the least of reasons for bass' popularity is that they are not picky about what they eat. If they are hungry they will thoroughly investigate about anything thrown in the water. If they are very hungry they will eat or try to eat various and sundry things such as birds not actually in though near the water's surface.

For example, one hot, sticky July day, Bill McCabe, of Marion, and I were fishing Lake Mermet, an Illinois Department of Conservation lake near Karnak, when a blackbird landed on a limb of a leafless bush standing in the water. The unsuspecting bird was no more than a foot or so above the surface when suddenly the lake exploded with a bass leaping for it. Fortunately for the bird and McCabe it was far enough away to avoid being clutched by the bass and flew away. Within a couple of seconds, McCabe's surface Lunker Lure flew toward that bush. The fish immediately attacked and literally engulfed it, and McCabe brought to the boat a bass weighing nearly five pounds.

It is widely accepted that the reason bass find plastic worms so interesting is because they don't hesitate to feed on snakes, particularly young ones. Southern Illinois lakes, and those farther south, are not natural habitats for real live nightcrawlers, so most bass have never seen the real McCoy. Frogs, mice, minnows, virtually any and all creatures of a size compatible with the large mouth of bass become victims of some bass somewhere. In Minnesota frogs are so popular for bass fishing that "frog kids" who catch and sell them to fishermen earn substantial spending money.

Bass not only take artificial lures with slam-bang abandon but also smack an impressive variety of lures on the surface to depths often down to 30 and even 50 feet. It is doubtful that if bass were not such leaping, twisting acrobats above the surface that their popularity would have reached such undeniable proportions. Bass' performance is more or less dependable, especially on the part of fish weighing from one to about four pounds. These fish break the surface, go airborne, plunge, and swirl perhaps two, three, or more times. The largest of the species seldom vault completely clear of the water, though most big fish will come up and thrash with huge mouths agape. It's enough to send cold chills creeping down your spine.

Within the array of freshwater game fish species the bass is not large, not small, fitting comfortably somewhere in between. The world-record largemouth black bass is 22 pounds 4 ounces, and the Illinois state record is, as of this writing, 13 pounds 1 ounce. In recent years some of the largest of this species have been caught in California, and these fish weighing from 18 to more than 20 pounds were of the transplanted Florida subspecies *Micropterus salmoides floridanus*. To identify specifically the Illinois largemouth black bass species just leave off the *floridanus*.

Unfortunately, Illinois does not contain bass powerful enough to yank you screaming out of a boat. The average bass caught in Southern Illinois weighs 2 pounds or less, but those ranging up to 10 pounds are not uncommon. It is also the rare season which produces more than a couple honest-to-goodness, certified scale-weight 10-pound bass. We know that on occasion fishermen tease a little by warping the truth. This is because they dislike dealing with all those confusing fractions. It's easier to say that a bass weighing 4 pounds 6 ounces, when carried to the nearest high round figure, weighs an even 5 pounds. So a lot of 8-pound bass weigh 9 pounds, and a few 9 pounders manage to creep over the 10-pound mark.

Anyway, despite widely reported accounts of 10-pound Southern Illinois bass being boated in quantities as thick as hailstones, it isn't so. Over a 15-year record-keeping period while writing for the *Southern Illinoisan* newspaper, I marked only 13 fish topping 10 pounds. Obviously, I did not know of every bass caught in this region. Nevertheless, for every 10 pounder weighed on certified scales a dozen bass weighing 8 pounds or more were recorded, and those in the 7-pound class were, by comparison, relatively routine.

One reason a 10-pound bass in Southern Illinois is such a rarity is that generally the northern species of *Micropterus salmoides* doesn't live long enough in this region to attain this unusual size. Statewide, the average life-span of largemouth black bass is between five and seven years, give or take a few months. It also requires five or six years for the average Illinois bass to reach a weight of 5 pounds. By then the fish is declining, perhaps living through its final winter. The climate of Southern Illinois, however, is better suited than the rest of the state to longer growing seasons for its bass and other fish species. The comparatively temperate weather zone coupled with fertile water in which bass live serve to enhance growth. A few individuals grow big and bold, though these are the exceptions rather than the rule. The rule is that 5- and 6-pound bass in Southern Illinois are common as corn, while 9 and 10 pounders are not.

About 20 years ago you could count on one finger the lake most likely to give up a 10-pound bass. Little Grassy had the reputation, and rightly so, for its consistent production of especially heavy bass. Today, every lake in this region competes for big-fish honors.

Just as a small, elite group of Southern Illinois bass fishermen bask in the glory of having caught a 10 pounder, the ambition of the average angler across the nation is to catch one weighing just 5 pounds. Most never will attain this goal. One reason is because fish can't possibly grow as fast as they can be hooked and landed. So the odds of catching the heaviest fish in the lake are staggering compared to opportunities of hooking small fish. It's the law of probability. There are a lot more 1- and 2-pound bass than there are in the more desirable heavyweight classes.

Still another significant reason more trophy bass are not caught, anywhere, is the incredible number of people trying almost hourly to catch them. We would call this law of diminishing returns; each fish taken from a body of water is one less to be caught by someone else. You'll agree there are regiments of someone elses to canvass the same water you just vacated.

Have these multitudes had an adverse affect on the area bass populations? Far from it. Let's look backward 25 years to the middle of the so-called good old days of fishing when one seldom found more than one or two other boats out on a weekday. At that time Rend, Carlyle, and Kincaid lakes existed only as dreams, and Cedar Lake would be years away. Lake of Egypt was an infant and Devils Kitchen was the last of three lakes born to parent Crab Orchard National Wildlife Refuge. Of the older, established lakes there was Little Grassy and Crab Orchard, Lake Murphysboro, Mermet, Horseshoe, and a smattering of city reservoirs plus all the strip mine pit lakes. So no matter from which angle we view and evaluate the fishing potential of the early 1960s it was, compared to today, very limited in its scope.

Also worthy of consideration is the technical knowledge of fisheries biologists today compared to past decades. Because of its importance no fish is studied more by more scientists than the largemouth black bass. The facts about this fish occupying just one tiny niche in the mind of the average biologist would displace virtually everything known about them 25 years ago. Knowledge translates to efficient management of the resource. So perhaps those good old days were not so good after all, and perhaps we are now functioning as bass fishermen more smoothly than ever before because of all the foregoing developments and improvements.

While on this subject it would be remiss not to emphasize that paramount within new developments and improvements is the state of the art equipment and fish rearing techniques at Little Grassy Fish Hatchery south of Carbondale. The recently completed state hatchery at Sand Ridge is also geared for the increasing demand for fish for waters to be stocked.

Southern Illinois is unique in the Midwest because to my knowledge there is no other region which holds so many choices of lakes within such scant driving distance. For example, if you are centrally located around Benton, Christopher, or Du Quoin, in less than an hour you can be on Carlyle Lake at the extreme; Rend Lake is just minutes away; Crab Orchard, Little Grassy, Devils Kitchen, and Lake of Egypt are reached within 30 minutes; Lake Kincaid or Cedar Lake another 15 minutes; and Horseshoe Lake, at the outside, falls within a gently handled two-hour trip. This, of course, touches only those lakes known to have the longest shorelines. It does not begin to blanket all of the water available within an hour's drive of the centrally located angler. And this is what makes this region unique or nearly so. This also means that despite the tremendous popularity of bass fishing in Southern Illinois the diversity in size and location of lakes helps to distribute the fishing pressure instead of concentrating it on one specific bass population.

Not to be overlooked is the notable lack of sameness of fishing techniques required on these various lakes. No matter how subtly different the characteristics of each may appear to be there is a substantial difference from lake to lake. An illustration of this would be the fisherman who knows the hidey hole of every bass group in the Herrin City Reservoir. This does not mean that the same person will experience the same success by spending just a day or two casting for bass in less familiar nearby water such as Lake of Egypt, Devils Kitchen, or Little Grassy. Each one presents a little different puzzle to be sorted out.

About 90 percent of catching fish is in knowing where they are in a given body of water. The balance is in being there with a lure in the water at the right time. Jim Aaron once commented that catching bass is no more than time versus fish. When one knows where they are located within a lake, usually this remains unchanging, so it's a matter of then spending time to catch them.

When a given body of water holds a stable bass population the person who concentrates efforts fishing familiar water will, in all probability, find greater success than when going from lake to lake. The immense acreage of some lakes notwithstanding, imagine, if you will, that each contains no more than a series of pond-size spots where bass congregate. Also form the image that near your home are four farms and on each is a pond stocked with bass. In a single morning you can visit all four ponds, driving from one to another. This, then, is exactly how bass groups are distributed in all lakes of all sizes.

Most bass do not roam far from the proximity of the shallow water where they were spawned and hatched. The distances these bass travel can be measured in yards. Their lifestyle includes going deeper, staying there longer as they gain length and weight. This is because small bass up to a pound or so find compatible-sized food in shallow water. As they grow, food size becomes less problematic; they can eat about any prey which won't skedaddle out of range at the sight of them.

On the other hand, studies with telemetry show that a few are great travelers, tracked with these electronic devices astonishingly farther than their stay-at-home kin. Perhaps this is because nature abhors a vacuum. She prefers that every available portion of suitable habitat be utilized. Wildlife and fish populations, particularly those in abundance, often venture to establish new territories, filling these voids.

But can too much fishing pressure harm individual populations of bass? Irrevocably, yes. There are far too many case histories proving this has happened to believe otherwise. Perhaps excessive pressure alone will not completely render a population irreplaceable in time by its own natural means, though enough harm can be done that fishing results become nearly null and void. And show me a person who really believes that at least occasionally a fish should not be caught in order to sustain an interest in this sport and I'll be looking at a troubled person who enjoys spending vacations in a laundromat.

In order to keep pace with the ever-changing times, over the decades regulations governing daily catch limits of bass have also changed. In the 1940s fishing season was closed statewide during the spring spawning period; June 1 was the annual opening day. Then, it was agreed amongst fisheries folk that closing the season served no worthwhile purpose affecting bass populations. Fishing for them was thrown wide open year-round, remaining to this day. Meanwhile, the legal daily catch limit of 10 bass went unchanged until the late 1970s when it was reduced to 6 bass per day. The reason it was reduced was that steadily increasing fishing pressure was having an adverse effect on populations in a number of Illinois lakes.

Furthermore, a few designated waters were assigned a minimum legal length of bass permitted to be kept by fishermen. All these regulations are significant in the overall plan to safeguard the resource while providing the ultimate in quality fishing. When we examine the six bass per day limit we come up with the conclusion that for most of us fishing anytime, anywhere, six fish is an unattainable goal for which to shoot. We might just as well unrealistically try to collect a Canada goose dinner by shooting at a 500-yard range. Examining more closely the minimum 14 inch bass limit on a few lakes doesn't necessarily arouse any great fear these waters will be fished stone dry of their bass. As mentioned elsewhere a sound-bodied 14 incher is in its prime of life and will exceed 2 pounds.

Someone much wiser than I am once said that a fish taken from the water for food is worth about 50 cents per pound. The same fish in the water is worth about 50 dollars as an object for sport fishermen. Obviously, a lot more money is spent in the pursuit of fishing than there is in the actual catching. Equally obvious is that that old adage was coined when the price of fish was a helluva lot cheaper than it is today.

Opposite the person who keeps all fish of all sizes from all waters is the one who, for reasons not perfectly clear to me, refuses to keep bass of any size. If releasing every bass makes him feel warm and con-siderate of his fellow anglers, then he is misguided. It is scientifically unrealistic and naïvely optimistic to believe that all bass of all ages are going to be around long enough to be caught again by anyone. It doesn't work that way.

Naturally, we can be reasonably certain that a one-pound bass put to death will not reach maturity and reproduce following the date of its demise. But can we be equally certain that the average six-pound bass of advanced age, approaching that silvery waterway leading to that big structure in the sky, will not be as dead as last year's calendar this time next week? The average bass this age is nearly at the end of its natural life-span. It is of no biological consequence affecting the fish population when senior citizen bass die. This, like the spring spawn, is routine and although no one knows how many bass nation-wide die of old age it must be many thousands, perhaps millions. This is why I have to wonder about those who hysterically rant against anglers who keep these exceptionally large old bass with dusty gray scales at their temples. Bass age two have the capacity to reproduce, so all things being equal they have in their average life cycles three to five years to procreate. It makes sense, then, to guard the welfare of these young to middle age fish by not being greedy.

For example, myself and two others unknowingly virtually stripped clean a small pond of its fishable bass population. When we had finished with this three-acre pond there were so few catchable bass left in it that finding one was a major chore. Patrick and Barbara Terry own the farm land and pond in question situated about midway be-tween Carbondale and Murphysboro. I had known them for many years, fished their pond regularly, and both of them also enjoy this sport. They especially enjoy the handy source of fresh fish, and a pending fish fry was the reason for the described onslaught.

Friends of many years, Bill and Wanda Stone, of Urbana, were visiting my wife, Melba, and me. On a previous visit the Stones had met the Terrys, and the subject of a fish fry came up. The Terrys would provide the fish, and all we had to do was catch them. Usually, this was no problem at the Terry pond. A day later, Barbara Terry, Bill Stone, and I teamed up to catch the basics for the meal. Patrick Terry was off doing whatever farmers do on tractors.

The majority of bass in this pond were in the two-pound group, a voracious size often with insatiable appetites. It was also one of those rare days when all conditions were nearly ideal, so few casts of spinner baits failed to be stopped by a bass. So quickly were enough bass stockpiled for the dinner that our welling adrenalin had not peaked out, when Barbara echoed our combined thoughts. From about 50 yards down the shoreline she called, "Keep right on fishing, and I'll freeze all extra fish." There were a lot of extra fish, about two dozen. In fact we left so few that in following weeks scarcely a fish of this age group could be found.

The Terry pond did not begin to recover for nearly two years when younger bass grew large enough to fill this wide chasm. Recovery was painfully slow because in our ignorance at the time we caught and killed the majority of an age group coming into the most prolific reproduction time of its life.

The annual lifestyle and reproduction cycle of black bass is sufficiently pertinent to give it a thorough observation. With our eyes on the reality of what is happening down there in bassdom, the less perplexing this unpredictable species becomes.

A bass is a bass no matter where in Illinois, the nation, or the world it is found. Its habits, habitats, and need for food are the same everywhere. Most of the year bass live in or near deep water. In the hottest summer weeks it is not unusual to find them 30 to 50 feet deep. Bob Reeves, my son Steve, and I, all of Carbondale, caught bass in the gin-clear water of Lake Yojoa in Honduras down to 60 feet, and 35 to 40 feet were average daylight fishing depths.

The only two objectives in life for bass are to eat and reproduce. In spring they are motivated by both and these instincts are stimulated by rising water temperature. Shallow, quiet water warms faster than deep, wind buffeted areas, so bass migrate to the shallows.

We must remember, too, that as cold-blooded creatures bass and other fresh-water fish have body temperatures the same as the water in which they live. Their body temperatures fluctuate only as much as the rising or falling temperature of the water. Very cold bass are relatively inactive—in winter feeding only enough to stay alive. Warm bass and other fish are extremely active, taking food regularly and gaining weight and length.

In spring nearly every lake has layers of water with various temperatures. The deep water holes where bass have lived all winter may be around 40 degrees; the mid-depth water could be significantly colder, say about 35 degrees; and the surface, which is warmed by the spring sunshine, is the warmest water of all at 45 degrees. Naturally, continued sunny days will cause the surface temperature to rise much faster than those of the mid-depth or bottom water levels. This warming water is what draws bass upward to feed and to prepare for the spawn. Taking food has priority until the water temperature is high enough to be compatible with the particular spawning requirements of this species.

Just before bass spawn is one of the easiest of all times to catch them. It is relatively easy because they are accessible to fishermen who cast lures to shallow water shorelines, to the inundated stumps, sunken logs, brush, grass, and weed beds. These are the objects bass rise to and hide near in order to ambush small prey fish. A most important spring temperature range of shallow water is 50 degrees to 60 degrees. At 50 degrees or so bass are physically able and willing to feed actively, and as the temperature steadily climbs they become increasingly active, taking food and making ready to spawn.

As we have seen, bass are totally object-oriented particularly when they are in relatively shallow water. They like to snuggle up close to anything which has a marked difference from their own body shape. If there is a single, isolated stick in evidence poking above the surface the unseen portion beneath the surface may be enough to attract and hold the heaviest bass in the lake.

In spring the first movement of bass from deep to shallow water is toward the entrances to coves and protected bays. Their purpose is twofold, finding something to eat and later to spawn in these same areas off the main body of water. Usually, small male bass are first to penetrate cove areas. These fish search for and choose nesting sites, build the nests, and later guard the eggs and fry.

Meanwhile, large females heavy with roe generally hole up at cove entrances, staying secluded near objects on or near points where they feed at every opportunity. If this includes going for an artificial lure only resembling something edible, bass give it not a second thought. Their ability to think is about as developed as the thought process of a light bulb. It illuminates only when switched on, and the switch to the brain of bass is showing them something to put in their belly. Now, off those points near coves and just inside bay entrances are the places one is most likely to catch very healthy female bass. This is especially so as water temperature nears 60 degrees.

For this species ideal egg hatching temperature is 62 degrees and above. This means, of course, that bass instinctively try to take full advantage of a water temperature nearing this ideal. To do this males busy themselves selecting and preparing nests, fanning with their tails depressions in the bottom where eggs will be deposited. Depending on the specific nest site, clarity of water, and the size of bass these round-shaped nests may be at depths ranging from a couple feet to six or ten feet. In my experience at no time during the annual life cycle of black bass will males be more pugnacious, protective, and downright surly than while they choose and construct nest sites.

This is also one of those rare times when bass will race more than a couple of feet or so to intercept and attack a supposed intruder. Nest builders, as though bound to this commitment at any cost, often charge furiously for yards to impart their violence on lures. Although many veteran bassing people scoff at the notion that one can actually see a distinct V-shaped wake on the surface as a bass recklessly slashes toward a lure, it does happen. More often than not this happens when surface lures are used, and these surface lures, in particular, will be buzzbaits such as the Lunker Lure.

When seeing this awesome wake the natural tendency, like seeing a golf ball whizzing at you, is to duck out of its way. Fortunately for the fisherman, however, the speed of the bass doesn't allow anything more than taking a posture of self defense. Usually, this includes lurching backward, which luckily also sets the hook. All this makes excellent fodder for grandiose stories told and retold at the bar while pointedly omitting, of course, the part about damn near hurling yourself backward out of the boat.

Prespawn females also move savagely, especially when they slam surface lures, leaving no doubt what has happened. One warm spring evening on Crab Orchard Lake my wife, Melba, and I caught three bass in five casts covering a weed bed no larger than a pool table. All were large females. The heaviest weighed more than seven pounds and the smallest went four. This balmy evening the surface temperature was 59 degrees, and the bass were suspended within these weeds.

Across the bay fishing a small cove was Paul Barnwell, of Marion, and later when we touched base Barnwell told me that he had also caught a seven pound bass. He had watched, in fact, as Melba and I caught those three fish. Importantly, this same April morning we had fished this same location with the same lures without getting a ripple of a reply from this or any other spot on the lake. Bass were not in the shallows that morning. Following a full day of brilliant sunshine the surface had warmed enough, and a bass migration to the shoreline weed beds took place. So here, within sight of each other, we have two boats catching large bass nearly at the same time, and Barnwell already had caught a couple of smaller fish before entering the cove where we saw him.

Perhaps the strongest evidence of mass migrations of bass from deep to shallow water occurred during a 1970s tournament on Crab Orchard Lake. It was April and the weather had been cool to chilly. The frequency of bass found near shorelines had been at best very erratic. One day before this contest began, however, temperatures soared under sunny skies. But while on the first contest day shoreline casters scored with many fish, their counterparts who concentrated on deep water caught the majority of better fish. That night, unbeknown to the contestants or anyone else for that matter, happenings beneath Crab Orchard's surface would result in a complete turnaround. It appeared that suddenly every bass in the lake was in shallow water.

Consequently, the second day those who returned to deep water holes caught no or few bass, though shoreline fishermen scored heavily. Equally important, there was a full moon during this tournament, and bass did migrate under the brightness of this moon. This is the typical spring occurrence. Bass ready to enter shallow water to feed and spawn found, literally overnight, all conditions ideal.

Again, it is common behavior for bass to group near spawning sites while deeper inside these coves males make ready to search out females, guiding them to nests. When both are situated over the depression, eggs are dropped by the female while being fertilized by the male. With her work complete the female leaves the site. The male stays on to guard the cluster of eggs from predators and also dutifully to oxygenate the spawn by fanning his tail over the eggs. When this process takes place under those theoretically ideal conditions, which generally occur only in fish hatcheries, eggs hatch their swarming dark mass of fry in about 72 hours.

It is during the period between the actual laying of eggs by females and the following days as males protect the hatched offspring that bass fishing is not worthy of its name. This time is better spent puttering around the house with long-delayed chores. Generally, this annual doldrum sets in the latter days of April into May.

Following the egg-laying process, females take time to recuperate, so they are inactive and nearly uncatchable. At this same time male bass are so busy guarding nests, chasing away bluegill, crappie, and other species that would eat the eggs, and fanning their tails over the nests that they do not feed.

The male's responsibility is no less demanding when the eggs hatch. Now, a few thousand tiny bass form a restless black cloud weaving, ever swirling, just beneath the surface. Their parent tries to keep them in check, herding them like cattle, cutting them off at the pass when they stray too far. The rustlers are waiting out there, too. Most young bass never see their first birthday. Most will not see the end of the month. A heavy percentage will not live through their first week. Predators account for an incredible number of fry.

Roy Heidinger, who is regarded internationally as one of the foremost authorities on the black bass species, told this writer years ago that perhaps only 1 or 2 percent of a bass spawn survive to grow into adult fish. The Carbondale scientist also emphasized that for even this small number of fish to survive past the fry stage conditions must be good to excellent. This makes sense. Depending on the size of the egg-laying female there can be in each bass nest from 5,000 to 50,000 or more eggs. If all of them survived we would be up to our rear bumpers in squirming bass.

Young bass can also be their own worst enemy; if they are not eaten by larger fish they eat each other. It is common for bass just a couple inches long to suddenly discover their cannibalistic instinct. They turn on each other with the speed of a striking rattlesnake. If this were not enough to fret over, there is also that worrisome parent to watch from the corner of an eye. Day by day the male grows hungrier, becomes disenchanted with this whole affair, and like as not in one swift movement will turn on the mass of fry and gulp down as many as he can, then leave the rest to fend for themselves. The next time he sees any of them, if he does, it will be through the eyes of a cannibal viewing the smaller fish as a meal, nothing more.

Generally the last of May and first days of June again provide excellent fishing, but this time bass will be away from shorelines, off the points and drop-offs near their year-round home bases. Because the water temperature is compatible with optimum activity, bass feed regularly throughout the summer. This regularity doesn't change until late fall when water temperatures drop again, and bass feed with a flurry preparing for the long winter back in deep holes.

During the coldest weeks the metabolism of bass slows, and their food intake is minimal because they don't need a great amount to survive. In winter, bass become dormant as opposed to true hibernation; they rouse themselves only when necessary to find food, so it's common to catch them through ice. Perhaps bass use warm winter days to come from the depths to search for food.

White Bass.   Perhaps we can clear up confusion about the bass and sunfish families. The white bass is a true bass while the largemouth black bass, as already mentioned, is a member of the sunfish family. The yellow bass, striped bass, and hybrid striped bass are related to the white bass. With the largemouth black bass in the sunfish group are smallmouth and spotted bass, crappie, bluegill, redear, etc. Of the true bass group in Southern Illinois the white bass is best known, widely distributed, and has been around longer than the striped or hybrid striped bass crossed with white bass.

One school of white bass can provide enough thrills to talk about all summer. These are wolf packs of the lakes hunting down gizzard and threadfin shad. When they find them near the slick surface on a quiet day the lake literally erupts dozens of miniature geysers as white bass slash through the leaping, darting shad. As this takes place, white bass can be heard for many yards slurping down minnows with sounds like a powerful vacuum cleaner sucking up pieces of paper.

White bass especially prey on young gizzard shad of up to a couple inches in length. They wildly gorge themselves until there is not enough space left in their stomachs to hold a BB pellet. These fierce attacks on shad come at any time of day, so the fishermen who know what to look for, how to recognize these eruptions, go quickly to the spot and cast any medium to small size lure resembling a minnow.

By trophy standards the white bass is not a large species. The Illinois record is 4 pounds 14 ounces, and the world record is only 5 pounds 9 ounces. But we do not have a fish that slams a lure harder than white bass. And the average weight of white bass in Illinois does not reach 1 pound.

Setting the time when Southern Illinois anglers first realized that white bass had been introduced also pinpoints an era when few people knew what they were. This was 1967, and Crab Orchard Lake was the site of this confusing discovery. Experimental stocking of white bass had earlier been due at Crab Orchard. Obviously, they thrived on the gigantic population of gizzard shad. Nonetheless fishery biologists who introduced these fish remained tight-lipped about the experiment, biding their time until they knew one way or another how it fared. It fared very well, thank you, and by 1967 the white bass population had increased to the very catchable stage both in quantity and individual size. Summer fishermen exposed the closely guarded secret. While fishing for black bass on the midlake channels and drop-offs people like Al Peithman suddenly started hauling in white bass. One right after another. The fearless little whites had no compunction whatsoever about taking on large bass lures. One day, Peithman, struggling under the burden of an awesome stringer of white bass, amazed Bill Harkins and me at the boat dock. "Whatever they are," Harkins said, "you've sure got a bunch of 'em. I hope they're good to eat." "Yeah," Peithman said dryly. "But what are they?"

I had seen only photos of white bass, never one dressed in its natural scales, and except for color these held a striking similarity to yellow bass. But compared to these fish the yellow bass in Crab Orchard were small. It was rare to catch one more than six or seven inches long. I suggested that maybe, just maybe, they could be white bass. Both Peithman and Harkins fixed me with a blank stare. "I don't know that they are," I shrugged, "but they fit the description." "Whatever," Peithman said, "I couldn't keep a Bomber away from 'em. They jumped it every cast. I've never caught so many fish so fast in all my life!"

They were white bass, of course, and from that day forward we started looking for them to show up on those same open lake drop-offs. When they did occasionally appear it was just as Peithman had said—it was impossible to cast without a strike. If Alexander Graham Bell had invented a means of communication as swift as the fisherman's grapevine he would have died a happier man. Curiosity about this "new" hard-hitting fish brought scores of fishermen down on Crab Orchard. It didn't take long before experienced anglers knew what to expect of white bass.

White bass in Southern Illinois usually spawn in late April or early May. Their preferred spawning grounds are in the small streams or rivers feeding lakes. When substitute spawning sites are necessary they use sandy, rocky places such as riprap on shorelines. By late May or early June they are back in the lake in large schools roaming the shallow areas looking for young of the year gizzard or threadfin shad.

July is an excellent month to fish for white bass as they forage on shad. On windless mornings when even roosters suffer guilt for shattering the tranquillity, the expectant observer may see uprisings of shad boiled skyward by dozens of white bass gorging on them. In some lakes these puffs of watery spray might cover a half acre or more.

But we don't have to rely on visual contact with surface-feeding white bass in order to catch them. Find where they live and they can be caught daily for weeks on end. On Rend Lake, for example, there is a place of bottom structure which holds white bass like a magnet. This is a long bar or inundated islandlike hunk of bottom about 12 feet deep on top and slopes down to 14 and 15 feet on either side. By drifting or trolling along this bar, keeping a lure very near the bottom, schools of white bass are not difficult to find.

Trolling deep-running lures is one of the most efficient methods of locating white bass. When that first contact is made, toss out a floating marker with a line and weight to keep it anchored to that spot. Now, swing the boat around and retrace your path nearly brushing against the marker. When second contact is made with fish quickly heave out the second float, and you have the rascals completely surrounded. Troll between the two marks, or if you prefer, anchor and cast. The described Rend Lake location of white bass habitat is not an isolated example. In Carlyle and Kincaid lakes and nearly all waters where white bass are found there are places where, in summer, fishing deep structures is extremely profitable.

Generally, medium to small lures are best, though this is not necessarily the case all the time. We have to recall how white bass first, accidentally, were discovered to be in Crab Orchard Lake. The 500 series Bomber is a large lure. Lures used for casting to surface white bass can be anything you can manage to get out of the boat. When caught up in a frenzy white bass don't care who made the lure or what it's called. If the lure has weight enough to reach the action and will sink below the surface it will catch fish. Reliable hardware, however, to have on hand are minnowlike crankbaits in the alphabet series, spinner baits, Bagley's Bass'n Shad, Cotton Cordell's Stay'n Shad, the Rebel Double Deep Shad or any similar lures, and, of course, small Bombers.

Trolling deep is a different approach, so we must hang out lures that will get down there and probe the bottom. Most of the aforementioned lures in larger sizes will do this as will many other brand names and types. Rather than to use this space to suggest which brand names to buy, suffice it to say that most minnowlike lures scraping near bottom will appeal to the predator instincts of white bass.

The advantage of knowing a few summer bases of whites comes at a time when fishing for other species begins to slow. Many a good intention of looking for largemouth bass has been interrupted by schooling white bass at the surface exploding shad like shrapnel.

Common names for white bass include silver bass, silver fish, and striped bass, though the latter should not be used because there is an altogether separate striped bass in Southern Illinois. The name "silvers" is very common throughout the white bass belt. For instance in Central Indiana where white bass have been around for 30 years or more there's a phrase to describe their surface activity. Fishermen here say that, "The silvers are firing!" This is a very apt description. White bass can turn a smooth lake into a roaring prairie fire.

Striped Bass. Freshwater striped bass were accidents looking for a place to happen. It happened in South Carolina in 1941 in lakes Marion and Moultrie which are part of the Santee-Cooper impoundment projects. Until then the striped bass, also known as rock fish, was considered a saltwater species that used rivers and brackish waters to spawn. No one suspected this fish could become so easily adapted to freshwater, so it was totally unexpected to find them in Marion and Moultrie.

By chance striped bass were in the feeder rivers spawning when the dams to these impoundments were closed, locking off their routes back to the sea. Like our white bass in Crab Orchard Lake, no one knew they were there until a few stripers began showing up on fishermen's stringers. Unlike our white bass, however, even the fisheries biologists of South Carolina were not aware of stripers being in the Santee-Cooper reservoirs, and they were the most ecstatic of all to learn of their presence.

Even more heartening were the striper age groups, which meant they were spawning successfully in these lakes. A striper spawn is an involved process unlike that of freshwater fish species. They leave saltwater, to go up rivers and spawn. The eggs float on the current toward the sea. Generally, within 72 hours the eggs hatch their fry, which means that a float of perhaps of 50 to 100 miles has been covered.

Meanwhile, stripers in the Santee-Cooper were growing big and bold and smashing up a lot of flimsy tackle, and had been caught purposefully or by accident from the two impoundments. By that time the nation was aware of the phenomenon. Here was a saltwater fish that could and did grow to 50 pounds or more in freshwater, a fish that was content enough to gobble down gizzard shad as it did saltwater crabs or mullet, and it would zero in on artificial lures with the same reckless abandon as schooling white bass. Obviously, the nation wanted striped bass.

At first it wasn't easy to get them. Stripers would not spawn just any old place. Conditions had to be right, so artificial conditions were orchestrated by South Carolina fisheries scientists. From these hatcheries came the eggs and fry which stocked dozens of lakes throughout southern states.

It was also inevitable that many states would build their own striper rearing facilities. Fisheries scientist Roy Heidinger did this in Southern Illinois. It was a state of the art hatchery designed specifically for the exclusive raising of striped bass. Fish from this facility near Gorham would be stocked in lakes throughout the state.

Years prior to that time, however, a very bizarre series of occurrences gave us a clue that Crab Orchard Lake, again, was being used experimentally. Evidently, biologists figured that if a fish could live in Crab Orchard it would thrive anywhere else. One day before the first clue surfaced that striped bass were in Crab Orchard, I received a call from James Burgess, of Herrin, who said that he had just caught what might be the new state record white bass. Would I check to see what the record was. I would and did, and at that time it was 4 pounds

4 ounces or thereabout. Indeed, Burgess said his fish topped the record by 3 or 4 ounces! He would have it reweighed on another certified scale just to make sure of the exact poundage. Virtually assured of being officially credited with a state record fish, Burgess followed instructions to the letter, with the certified scale weight with witness signatures, plus the black and white glossy photos of the fish taken personally by the author. This documentation was submitted to the Illinois Department of Conservation.

Meanwhile, however, there were disturbing factors about this whole episode. I had the nagging suspicion in a corner of my mind that the Burgess description of how he caught the white bass was strange, completely out of character for this species. Yet, his physical evidence was undeniable. This was a magnificent white bass. Burgess had said that he was casting a Lunker Lure for black bass in shallow water weed beds in a cove on Crab Orchard Lake when the white bass pounded the lure. His wife was with him in the boat, and she verified his every word. But, I was amazed that a white bass would act this way, be found in such a place, and hit a surface lure as it did.

In due time, and as fully expected, the fish caught by Burgess was admitted as a new state record white bass, and everyone involved was pleased to have been a part of it. Remember, too, in order for the fish to be officially certified all evidence submitted to the state had to be carefully examined by qualified persons who make these judgments.

A year passed with the Burgess record intact. Then, a second occurrence on Crab Orchard gave a lot of people sufficient reason to ponder. Two Du Quoin fishermen came up with a mystifying catch on their trotline set for catfish. This fish was identified as a striped bass, and it weighed 22 pounds! This unsettling information must have sent record keepers scrambling to review data, and it wasn't the 22-pound striped bass they were concerned about. It was out of the question for this large striper to be even considered for record honors. All game fish species must be caught with rod and reel, so the trotline-hung striped bass didn't qualify.

A few weeks later Jim Burgess called to discuss his state record white bass for the second time. "You'll never guess what happened," he said. "My record fish was just revoked." Revoked? How in the hell can a state record be recalled, I wondered. Why? "Now, they say it's not a white bass at all, it's a striped bass, one of those bastards that get huge," he said bitterly. "They made a mistake in identification, so my record is wiped out." And so it was, just like that, according to Burgess.

As explained by the Crab Orchard Refuge manager, Arch Mehrhoff, the truth of the matter was that in 1966 a U.S. Fish and Wildlife biologist had stocked striped bass in Crab Orchard Lake. As nothing more had been heard about them for years he assumed they didn't survive, so they were forgotten. At least two of them did survive. The 22 pounder caught by the Du Quoin men and the "white bass" landed by Jim Burgess.

It is ironic that in the midst of all this confusion a Mounds woman caught a 16-pound striped bass in a backwater off the Ohio River. This fish established the first state record for the species. As this book goes to press the current state record stands at 19 pounds 6 ounces, caught by James Patton from the Saline River in Gallatin County.

For all the foregoing and much to follow is the reason I said earlier that perhaps it is best to not refer to white bass as stripers or striped bass; they are separate species of the same family group. As it is there is more than enough bewildering confusion about their identification. To the untrained eye of the layman it is easy to mistake one for the other, particularly when both are about the same size and roughly the same weight as the average white bass in Southern Illinois. The marked difference between species is that white bass stripes do not flow unbroken in a solid line, while these same markings on a striped bass generally are distinct solid lines from near the head to the tail. Still another difference is that on the back of the white bass's tongue is a single patch of teeth. In the same place the striped bass has two sets of teeth.

All of this sameness gave rise to the "wiper," which is a hybrid cross between white bass and striper. This fish usually takes on the solid line characteristics of the striped bass. There is a wide range of weight difference between the hybrid and the striped bass. A hybrid weighing 10 to 15 pounds is regarded as good, while the world-record striper weighed 59 pounds 12 ounces. This huge fish came from the Colorado River above Lake Havasu, which forms a portion of the border between Arizona and California. This same area has given up a number of striped bass of up to 50 pounds in recent years, making it one of the premier striped bass fisheries in the nation. While hybrids rarely exceed 20 pounds, striped bass of 20 to 40 pounds are not uncommon.

Stripers feed on so many different things at different times it is impossible to categorize them into a narrow band. They take live bait, cut bait, and artificials with equal voraciousness, frequently chase shad on the surface like white bass, and the occasional fish is not above hunkering in ambush to wallop a surface lure as evidenced by the previously discussed James Burgess striped bass.

Most manufacturers offer a variety of lures designed for stripers. These range from surface lures to deep trollers to heavy saltwater weighted jigs. But before loading up with all these special striper tools, the Southern Illinoisan should question whether the return justifies the investment. Stripers and hybrids here have adapted to existing food. In most lakes gizzard and threadfin shad are fish most often eaten by these predators. It would appear, then, that lures of this type commonly used for bass would get the job done on stripers and hybrids. An equally important consideration is that, in an area encompassing Lake Kincaid through Rend Lake, Lake Baldwin, and northward to Clinton Lake, there are only a handful of lakes containing stripers or hybrids. Crab Orchard, of course, is among them. Others are Collins Lake in Grundy County, Hillsboro New City Lake, and Stephen Forbes Lake near Kinmundy.

Perhaps more important than having special lures is the rod, reel, and line. The well-equipped bass caster is all set for stripers and hybrids as this tackle in most instances is adequate for the job. Spin fishermen should pay special attention to line strength. Should you chance to hook a bulldozing striper, a 20-pound test line will stand you in good stead. There is the possibility, of course, that even this won't be enough.

Stripers, hybrids, and white bass are not leapers. They don't jump out of the lake in exciting displays. But once hooked they will go thataway, fast, and line will leave the reel with dazzling speed. If you accidentally put your thumb on the whirling spool which is under pressure by a very large striper, you will feel a scorched agony. The striper is one fish that you don't want to mess around with by fruitlessly trying to land it prematurely. All this is what makes the landlocked striper such an exciting addition to Illinois.

Crappie. The average fisherman is not too concerned with correctly identifying either of the two crappie species. Except for slight coloration differences they are nearly identical. The white crappie has five or six spines in its dorsal fin and the black crappie seven or eight. Other variations require measuring, which most of us leave to skilled fisheries biologists while we get on toward our objective of cleaning and eating crappie. Included in the sunfish family, crappie is one of the most popular species in Southern Illinois. They are caught literally by the thousands if not millions.

Like the largemouth black bass, crappie are predators, so they readily take a variety of lures. It is not uncommon to catch crappie on lures designed for bass. Basically, crappies' goal in life is to find and eat minnows, which is the reason they are attracted to artificials resembling their more natural food. Many Southern Illinois lakes are ideal crappie habitat because they also contain gizzard and threadfin shad, primary food sources for this game fish. Between the two minnow species it is accepted that threadfin shad make the most desirable food because of their prolific life cycle and slow rate of growth.

Until recent years gizzard shad was the most common shad in Southern Illinois lakes, and, perhaps because it was, the growth rate of crappie and other predator species suffered accordingly. Gizzard shad can reach lengths of 12 inches or so and may weigh as much as two or three pounds. Small crappie do not match the growth rate of this food they are supposed to eat, so crappie soon find themselves out of a source. Consequently, many lakes are plagued with an overabundance of stunted crappie. Being a hardy species, gizzard shad are not affected by winter water temperatures, and they reproduce plentifully, providing some food for small predators. Then, the shad growth rate outraces that of its predators and the predators virtually go hungry in the midst of plenty. Small bass in these lakes were equally affected. There was a time in Crab Orchard Lake when it took an incredible three to four years for the average bass to reach 1.5 pounds or so!

In many southern states, however, there was another shad species, the threadfin, which does not grow as large as gizzard shad. This remarkable little forage fish also reproduces up to three times in a summer, and their offspring reproduce the first year. The introduction of threadfins in Southern Illinois lakes appeared to be the ideal solution. Here was a food source with a maximum size of four to five inches and their prolific reproduction rate would provide a size suitable for all ages of game fish.

The problem was, however, that unlike gizzard shad, threadfins could not stand bitter cold water. They suffered a complete die-off when temperatures dropped to about 45 degrees or so. The use of threadfins in Southern Illinois seemed problematic. Fisheries biologist Roy Heidinger, head of the fisheries research center of Southern Illinois University at Carbondale, was convinced that threadfins would solve the food problem for game fish, particularly for crappie. His paramount hurdle was to solve the problem of the inevitable annual winterkill. The cost of acquiring and restocking threadfins each spring was prohibitive. Lake of Egypt south of Marion is a power supply impoundment with enough constantly flowing warm-water emission to sustain threadfins year-round, so Heidinger made arrangements for this lake to provide basic stocks of threadfins.

Because of its immense population of crappie, Crab Orchard lake was one of the first to be stocked by Heidinger with threadfin shad. This met with overwhelming success. Crappie gained remarkably fast. The average crappie was no longer the paper-thin specimen fishermen had grown accustomed to catching. These crappie were thick, broad, and robust. Naturally, every game fish in Crab Orchard and other lakes where threadfins have been introduced benefit from this food source. It is of no real consequence that each winter the majority of threadfin shad succumb to cold water. This is the inactive feeding period for all cold-blooded species, and they grow little or none at all. The critical weeks are summer when growth and weight gain are rapid for fish with sufficient nourishment.

Even so, the average crappie caught in Southern Illinois weighs less than a pound and measures eight to nine inches. Their life-span is roughly five years. There are, of course, many crappie heavier and longer than average. Two in particular were state records. The record black crappie was caught in May 1976 by John Hampton, of Christopher, as he fished Rend Lake. His huge fish weighed 4 pounds 8 ounces. The record white crappie, at 4 pounds 7 ounces, came from a farm pond near Jacksonville, caught in April 1973 by Kevin Dennis.

When these state records are compared with world records for the same species we begin to realize and appreciate just how large these Illinois crappie were and the potential for catching outsized fish. Hampton's black crappie was only 1.5 pounds shy of matching the world record, which is like catching a bass weighing more than 20 pounds! The Dennis white crappie was even closer, just 12 ounces off the world record.

The spring spawning period is one of the best times to fish for crappie. They are relatively shallow-water spawners, usually no deeper than about six feet or so, which makes them very accessible. If there is a best time to use small spinner lures and the well known "crappie jigs," this is it. When they are found near the weeds or brushy shorelines the person using artificials has a far greater chance of catching more fish than the minnow fisherman because of the time involved. The lure user can cast, hook, and land a couple crappie while the bait fishermen rigs up for the first cast. But, unlike other species in the sunfish family, crappie are not great fighters, nor do they send a resounding thump telegraphed through the rod when they take a lure. One of their many common names is "papermouth" because their mouths are thin and easily torn by a hook. Too much pressure applied to this delicate membrane rips the hook free.

Of all fish in Southern Illinois, of all freshwater fish everywhere, crappie have more common names than any other species. One would think that largemouth black bass with its popularity would have more, but that is not the case. Bass have only a few, such as linesides, big mouths, and hogs or "hawgs," the last a name which always has turned me completely off. Instead of calling a bass bucketmouth, or whatever, I see nothing wrong with calling it what it really is. Crappie seldom are called what they really are. The names include calico bass, speckled crappie or just specks, strawberry bass, silver crappie, and why they are called "bachelor," I'll never know. Every region in most states has other common names for this species, until they number in the dozens.

No matter where they are found, this is the same fish and they are caught by the same methods. In spring crappie love brush, stumps, and weeds, but they are not the shallow-water fish most people think they are. Following the spawn they go back to deep water. In some lakes they are commonly found from 25 to 35 feet deep. They do come up to find minnows and insects, then they retire to deep water.

It is when they are in the comparatively shallow-water feeding stages that they are caught by most fishermen. Other anglers who know where and how deep to look among the submerged stumps and brush catch far more crappie for more hours of the day. Generally, crappie are regarded as slow feeders, so in summer when they are deep is the prime time to use live minnows. One approach is to

Bass hiding beside stumps find it almost impossible to ignore lures repeatedly presented over their heads. (Photograph by the author)

The lakes of Southern Illinois offer some of the most scenic and exciting fishing in the Midwest. (Photograph courtesy of Mercury Marine Corporation)

Resembling a Louisiana bayou lake, Horseshoe Lake near Cairo offers especially good fishing for crappie and bluegill. (Photograph by the author)

Using a sufficiently strong spinning line enables this Devils Kitchen angler to land a bass from among snags. (Photograph by Ron Hamberg)

The author with his heaviest Southern Illinois bass, which came from Crab Orchard Lake. (Photograph by Bill Harkins)

Although smallmouth black bass are scarce to nonexistent in most of Southern Illinois, a few are found in Lake Shelbyville. (Photograph by the author)

Fred Wasburn, of Carterville, shows why he is regarded as one of the most knowledgeable bass fishermen in Southern Illinois. (Photograph by the author)

John "Gino" Swetz, of Royalton, waits out a bass not ready to be landed. One reason bass are so popular is that they are spirited fighters. (Photograph by the author)

C. K. "Corky" Swain, of Carbondale, *right*, with a friend and a trio of striped bass, a species now found in a number of regional lakes. (Photograph by the author)

July through September is an excellent time to find large schools of white bass as they feed close to the surface on gizzard and threadfin shad. Virtually every cast results in a jolting strike. (Photograph by the author)

Fisheries biologist Mike Conlin, of the Illinois Department of Conservation, prepares to measure and weigh a channel catfish of larger than average size than that usually found in Illinois waters. The channel cat is an all-time favorite of many anglers. (Photograph by the Illinois Department of Conservation)

Carp often spawn in ankle-deep water, a trait of which bow fishermen take advantage. (Photograph by the author)

Twenty-eight-pound buffalo caught on a trotline by Robert Hoyle, of Johnston City. Buffalo of this size are usually taken by trotline or net.

park the boat directly above suspect places, then lower live minnows to find the level at which these fish are hovering.

One time I met a man named Brown who spent weekends with his wife fishing for crappie on Little Grassy Lake. As I recall, their home was in the East St. Louis area, yet they knew every crappie "tree" in Grassy. They went to these trees, tied the boat to an exposed limb, then simply lowered live minnows at gradually increasing depths among the myriad of branches. Sooner or later they discovered the desirable depth, which for the most part was 20 feet or deeper. Although this is a common method used by crappie fishermen what set the Browns apart were the numbers of fish they piled up. They averaged nearly 100 fish per day! And large or small they filleted every last one of them.

In many Southern Illinois lakes crappie are found in places where they are least expected to be. Remember, these lakes are impoundments which were creeks or rivers before they became lakes. There was a great deal of natural habitat in these original channels, and it is still there holding fish populations as it has for many years.

Earlier, I mentioned that in many places where bass are found there is also habitat for other game species. This includes crappie. Whether this preferred habitat is found 100 yards or a half mile from the nearest land, chances are schools of crappie are there. The serious crappie fishermen should give thought to going armed with a depth finder to locate some of this habitat. If the lake is one for which there are topographical maps, so much the better. At any rate don't be hesitant about breaking away from shorelines. More crappie during summer will be found out in the lake than near banks.

Let's go back for a minute to those gizzard and threadfin shad. The former is strictly an open-water species, schooling by the thousands. Other than when they spawn, they stay away from shorelines. If gizzard shad are to become crappie food, then crappie must go to open water. In many places where crappie already live out there off the points, islands, drop-offs, and channels, all they have to do is come straight up to find shad. The fisherman who locates these places and fishes straight down reaps a harvest of what can be called untapped schools of crappie.

While threadfin shad will frequent shallow water, this forage also spends a great deal of time coursing over wide expanses of lakes.

Clearly, it is not a matter of survival for crappie if they never come within reach of the shallow-water shoreline angler.

When all else fails try splatterpoling. This is a unique way of getting crappie's attention, bringing them up from deep water to a bait or lure. Splatterpoling is commonly used in the Deep South, though to my knowledge it has not caught on in Southern Illinois—probably because fishermen can't bring themselves to believe it works. But it does.

The success of splatterpoling is intricately aligned with the feeding of crappie and other game fish on gizzard or threadfin shad. First, the boated fisherman establishes a moderate trolling speed letting a lure or bait string out behind the boat. Now, the tip of the fishing rod is thrust at a comfortable angle just beneath the surface and whipped back and forth. This sets up a swishing, slashing noise similar to the sounds made by predator fish charging through schools of shad. When this sound reaches crappie they come up to investigate, and they find instead of a school of shad the lure or bait. In my judgment small spinners or jigs trailed behind the boat are more effective than live minnows if only because lures are more expedient, taking less time to handle.

Splatterpoling? Should you think that this is ridiculous, I felt the same, viewing my first experience with great skepticism. It was a late June, hot and humid on a Mississippi lake. Earlier my host had insisted that it wasn't necessary to start fishing before breakfast, so the sun was a glowing ball by the time we launched the boat. Within an hour I was a believer. There were a dozen nice crappie in the live well, and before noon we had more than two dozen to clean.

The makers of tackle must have had crappie in mind when they produced light-action spinning gear, particularly ultralight tackle. Whippy little rods are ideal for casting lightweight spinners and jibs. The fly rod, of course, is the ultimate in action whether used with live minnows and a cork or with wet flies. Trying to heave weighted jigs or spinners with one of these wands, however, will give you the creeps as these deadly missiles whistle past your ear like angry hornets. This is when having a partner with a sharp knife is indispensable. You'll need both to cut the hook from the back of your neck.

Bluegill. If you were to ask a dozen people which of the fish species was the first they caught, chances are that no fewer than ten would say bluegill. Once that early love affair is established, we don't lose our affection for this fancy little sunfish.

Perhaps the old saying is true, perhaps not, that ounce for ounce the bluegill is the strongest fish in freshwater. To my knowledge there is no proof for or against this common claim. It really doesn't matter. Some things are best left undiscussed. The 2 pound 10 ounce bluegill caught by Rip Sullivan, of Marion, in 1963 is still the record fish. When we reflect that the average bluegill in Illinois weighs fewer than 6 ounces, we readily see the incongruity of one as large and aged as Sullivan's fish.

Among the millions of bluegill caught each year even a true one pounder is rare in Illinois. A large one weighs 10 to 12 ounces. It is these fish that are typically measured from the tip of one's fingers to somewhere up the wrist. "Just about this long, they were," says the fisherman. "Every last one of 'em. Musta weighed a pound if they went an ounce." Bluegill fishermen are not given to overmodesty, nor do they dampen enthusiasm by putting many bluegill on the scales. As I said, some things are best left unknown.

The bluegill is everybody's fish; in my lifetime I have never heard a hint of scorn regarding this ramrod-tough little fighter. Like bass and crappie, it is just about everywhere and is adaptable to ponds and lakes in the frozen north as it is to those in the searing heat of the desert. Bluegill is nothing at all if not a welded balance of muscle action to resist the force of a fishing rod. Picture in your mind the shape of this fish. Its body is nearly as deep as its length. When it is hooked this exceptionally strong fish converts into a finely tuned machine dashing back and forth while using its platter configuration against the pull. It is as though you have hooked a motorized dinner plate. Considering that a darting little 6-ounce fish can start the adrenalin flowing, we have to wonder what catching the world-record 4 pound 12 ounce bluegill was like. The Alabama fisherman who did this probably thought he had hooked an infuriated skin diver.

To the delight of Southern Illinois fishermen this is one species we can't catch too many of. Bluegill have the often used capacity to spawn two to three times each season, and the number of eggs deposited in a nest by a single adult female may exceed 60,000. Although the number of surviving fish is only a fraction of this, there are enough, generally, to quickly throw the balance of the pond or lake out of kilter. Bluegill populations obviously need to be kept in check. Otherwise their habitat becomes saturated with undersize fish. Larger predators such as largemouth bass and adult crappie help to do this. Fishermen also do their part and one of the most productive times to do this is in spring.

In this region, the first two weeks of May is the beginning of the spawning season. Bluegill "colonize" their nests in shallow water bathed in sunshine. This fish is, in fact, the only one we have in this area which builds groups of nests so closely knit and so evident near shorelines. These nest groupings appear as shallow depressions scooped out by the fanning tails of male bluegill. Like other members of the sunfish family, bluegill choose the sunny shallows for a specific reason. Heat from sun and water is necessary to generate the temperatures that hatch eggs. With the right temperature, bluegill eggs hatch fry within five to ten days.

This also means that prior to this time colorful male bluegill will be in the shallows dutifully building those roundish nests, and when they are they'll pounce on an intruder quick as a flash. There is absolutely no better time in the year for excitement than when large males rise to a popping bug, multilegged spider, or dry fly cast with a fly rod to the quiet surface over one of these nests. Place one of these artificials there and action is assured. Repeated action is guaranteed. Cast the lure and allow it to rest unmoving. If nothing happens twitch it just a little, enough to give it a struggling lifelike appearance, then be prepared to set the hook. After one fish is landed, do it all over again.

What many bluegill fishermen do not realize is that while males are grouped up on these nests, adult females are nearby, perhaps in a little deeper water. These can be reached by fishing a wet fly, tiny spinner, or a live bait such as crickets or worms. In many instances the females are heavier bodied than the males!

Spring bluegill offer an advantage to the wader as well as to fishermen with boats. If the shoreline can be walked, nesting colonies can be spotted. Then it's a matter of wading to take up a comfortable casting position. No one need be left out of spring bluegill activity. Even if you are not inclined to wade, and there is casting room from the dry land, many spawning beds can be reached with fly line or spinning tackle.

The word "deadly" this or deadly that lure or bait for various species is overworked and generally overrated. In this case, however, to say that live crickets falling within reach of bluegill anytime of year are the deadliest of all baits is not to exaggerate, at least by much. Whether bluegill are on the spawning beds or 25 feet deep, crickets must be particularly juicy meals for them.

Living out on the Giant City Blacktop Road south of Carbondale are bluegill anglers who give an all-new meaning to the seldom heard phrase, "If it won't take a cricket it ain't a bluegill." This is rarely heard because I just made it up. C. K. "Corky" and Karen Swain don't talk that way at all. Nonetheless, they are bluegill chasers, spring, summer, and fall, and Corky, by all accounts an expansive man, is quick to tell you his impressive catch records. We are talking records showing that if fewer than 1,000 bluegill were caught in only a few weeks it was an unaccountably slow period. On a number of occasions, I've been with both Corky and Karen Swain, cinching up those little crickets to hooks, and caught so many bluegill in such a short time that we failed to realize how much cleaning was ahead. Then, the jolting reality of a 100 or more sent a shiver down our spines.

Although it is unquestionable that crickets placed in a spawning bed will catch a tremendous number of bluegill, I think that by using them at this time in place of poppers, bugs, and flies a great deal of the fun is lost. Bluegill perform magnificently with these artificials. When the first spawn has ended, bluegill go out to deeper water, staying there much of the time, and this is when they become hard to locate. The average fisherman doesn't probe deep enough. For example, it's common for the Swains to add a couple split shot sinkers to their lines in order to investigate anywhere from 15 to 25 feet of water with crickets as they drift with the breeze or ease the boat along with an electric trolling motor against the current. And at times 30 feet down will produce the first series of hits.

Bluegill are a great deal like crappie, running in large schools throughout the summer, and like bass they also associate in size groups. Large fish tend to stick together and small with small. The size of bluegill we catch tells us whether we are doing everything right or if there is room for improvement. Consistently catching young bluegill usually means that we are not getting bait or lures deep enough to levels where the filleting slabs are. Small fish frequent shallow water because here is where their food is found, and they use the protection of weeds and brushy places to hide from large predators. Remember, it is a jungle down there.

It strikes me that the epitome of flattery is when your name is mentioned and it is instantly recognized in direct association with a fish that is not a bass. The late Bud Rose was one of these rare people. Mention bluegill around Murphysboro and you also mention Bud Rose. Rose fished Lake Murphysboro most of the time, and he was a one-man conservation department, keeping the fish populations thinned better than by spreading rotenone. Like all astute anglers, Rose knew the habits and habitats of the species he fished for, so generally it was a question of how many rather than how to catch bluegill.

I fished Lake Murphysboro with Rose just once, and that day there was more water above the boat than beneath it. Then, as the morning progressed, the gray-flannel clouds gave us a break by scattering and the sun popped through. Despite the early rain we caught bluegill from spawning beds near shorelines, then even more fish after the sky partially cleared. It was as though the fish were taking advantage of increased heat to accelerate their nest-building activities.

In this respect nature has set critical limits on the reproduction processes of bluegill as well as of other freshwater fish species. Temperature and water conditions govern the success or failure of a spawning effort. A spawn can be wiped out by high-water conditions, siltation, plummeting temperatures, rapidly decreasing water levels or any combination of these. Illinois is famous for weather patterns causing these adverse conditions. It is reasonable to assume, then, that nature gives bluegill the opportunity to bring off multiple spawns in order to safeguard the species. If indeed this was the case she did a very good job of it. In most lakes and ponds bluegill face no danger of becoming extinct.

The greatest threat to the bluegill living near Zeigler was the probability of ending their careers in Mitch's Tavern. For many years Mitch's Tavern was known far and wide as the place to be for free fish washed down by not-so-free beer. It was a weekly ritual for the distaff half of Mitch's Tavern to provide by her own means and fishing tackle all the fish hungry customers could eat. Della Mitchell caught gobs of bluegill, and she also cleaned and deep-fried them once each week.

Obviously there is no way of knowing how many bluegill over the years passed over that counter to robust people with insatiable appetites for this winning combination of fish and beverage. It must have been tons! It is equally obvious that it is unlawful to sell or caused to be sold game fish in the state of Illinois, and bluegill is one of the gamest of all fish. Mitch's Tavern found no problem with this. There was no charge for fish and the price of beer remained static, never hiked on that particular evening.

The popular bait of live crickets has been discussed. There are other baits which bluegill find equally appetizing. Among them are red wiggler worms and nightcrawlers. The advantage of red wigglers over nightcrawlers is comparative size. Wigglers are small and skinny enough to be threaded whole on a hook. The fatter worms need to be pinched off in sections or they offer so much meal that a bluegill could gnaw on them for hours before reaching hooks.

Of all the bluegill I have seen others catch, heard of being caught, and personally accounted for over the nation, I'm convinced that day in and day out Southern Illinois specimens compare favorably with those found in most places. Reelfoot Lake in Tennessee, for example, does not produce bluegill averaging heavier than bluegill from Horseshoe Lake near Cairo. And there are many Southern Illinois lakes which will match bluegill coming from Horseshoe Lake. No matter where you go in North America, it will be rare to find a place that yields bluegill averaging a certified scale weight of one pound. If you should find such a place, please let me know, and I'll be almost incoherent with excitement until I get there.

Redear Sunfish.   There is so little more to be said about redear sunfish that has not already been said about bluegill that we'll make only a couple of pertinent observations. First, compared to bluegill, redears are relatively scarce throughout Southern Illinois. That's a shame, too, because this species is uniformly larger than bluegills. Nonetheless, most fishermen catch redears by accident while fishing baits deep for bluegill. Redears are not the surface feeders their cousins are.

In their first year redears are heavier and longer than bluegill the same age, and throughout life they do not relinquish this head start. Redears weighing three-quarters of a pound are common in many lakes, and in others they average a half pound. For example the average bluegill age five in Southern Illinois measures 7.8 inches compared to 9.2 inches for redear the same age statewide.

Here, "statewide" is an important word. Because of length of growing seasons there are great differences in sizes of fish the same age from Southern Illinois and other regions of the state. Illinois is almost 400 miles in length. There can be as much as five degrees difference in temperature every 100 miles, particularly in spring and early summer. For this reason the Illinois Department of Conservation compiles charts listing separate Northern, Central and Southern Illinois regions having different rates of fish growth. Although the DOC does not single out redear sunfish growth in these three zones, it does include bluegill in these divisions of the state. So, if statewide, which includes northern Illinois, redear sunfish average nearly two inches longer than bluegill the same age, it makes sense to assume that this fish born and reared here in the fertile waters of Southern Illinois should be the chunky type of specimens everyone would like to catch—as indeed they are.

Catfish

Channel Catfish. The channel catfish is variously called fiddler, whiskers, forktail, spotted cat, and other common names, but for this volume it will be called channel catfish, because that's its proper name. The Illinois-record channel catfish, weighing 30 pounds 8 ounces, was caught from a farm pond in Kane County. The world-record 58 pound channel cat, which came from the Santee-Cooper reservoirs, S.C., in 1964 has not been beaten.

Of the three largest catfish in Illinois the channel cat ranks third in size, overshadowed by blue and flathead catfish, yet, the widely distributed channel cat is by far the most popular of all catfish family members, including the bullheads. There are few ponds, lakes, and rivers in the state that do not contain generous populations of channel cats. For good reason. Taken on rod and reel this is one of the gamest of all game fish, and when caught by any other means, such as on trot lines, throw lines, bank lines, or by jugging, this fish provides delicious meat. Indicators of its popularity as a food fish are the numerous catfish rearing farms and ranches across the nation that deal exclusively with channel catfish supplied to restaurants. This industry grows larger each year. Meanwhile, there is as much or more time spent by as many or more people fishing for channel cats than for any other species except largemouth black bass.

As a group the catfish family has an undeserved reputation for eating about anything including bar soap and old rubber tires. They are especially attracted to repulsively smelly things such as cheese of the rankest order and malodorous blood baits. The truth is that the basic diet of the channel cat is nearly the same as that of the sunfish family members; other fish, crayfish, insects, worms, snails, and other common foods found in most waters are routinely eaten by catfish. After all, how often does a fisherman come along to offer channel cats a dose of high and mighty Billy Bob's Good Ole Redneck Cheese Balls saturated with fortified chicken blood? To be sure, this formula is a good one, though most channel cats will never realize it.

What we realize about channel catfish is that generally they feed at night. Generally, they spend days in deep water. This is about as specific as we can get because, like many other fish species, catfish often are unpredictable. I've seen the time when in late afternoon hours before dusk not more than a dozen baited hooks on jug lines would be thrown from the boat before channel cats had seized the first couple baits.

Another time midafternoon channel cats completely upset our schedule for filming a carefully planned TV program. We were with Jim Walker, of Carbondale, and party on a houseboat, and ample stocks of essential provisions had been laid in. Pepsi, Big Orange Drink, ice cream, things like that. The schedule called for being on the lake with daylight time to prepare all jugs, attach assorted line lengths and get them baited and set out from the 14-foot jonboat towed by the larger craft. We were certain that most of the action would take place after dark. We don't film TV shows in the black of night, so this was geared to begin about sunup the following morning, leaving plenty of time to enjoy those Big Orange Drinks and eat ice cream. I think it was Goo Goo Cluster.

The sun still was a metallic white ball, the air hot and sticky, and long shadows had not begun to form when a couple dozen jugs floated near the houseboat. One jug was not in a pattern with the rest. It was insistent upon going elsewhere and it was going at a remarkable speed for a nonmotorized hollow piece of plastic. The channel catfish that was hooked on this line was only the beginning. We hauled in so many of them that long before sundown our filming chores were over and there was more than enough footage to be used in a program. Everything else was anticlimatic. The anticipation of our carefully scheduled night on the lakes was dulled, and so we finished off the last Pepsi and went home.

On overcast days channel cats often react like other fish species, coming from deep water to the shallows to find food. So no one can make a flat statement that this species always feeds after dark or during the weakest light conditions. Fisheries biologists do know, however, that channel cats spawn in June and July in this region. They like water temperatures of about 75 degrees for spawning. According to information published by the Fisheries Division of the Illinois Department of Conservation, this catfish species is about 12 to 15 inches long when it first spawns. The number of eggs per female varies with its size and maturity. The minimum number of eggs is roughly 2,500 while the maximum ranges to 70,000. It takes between 6 and 10 days for the eggs to hatch, and they are guarded by the male, who also stays to look after the fry. The average life-span of the channel catfish in Illinois is about eight years, and the average size caught ranges between one and two pounds.

No small reason why the channel cat is so popular is because it can be caught by so many methods. The purest, for many, is the rod and reel. Other people are equally dedicated to many-hooked trotlines. Trotlines are fashioned with a series of evenly spaced, short, drop lines tied to one long line. Generally, this is secured near the bank or shoreline and stretched across the water. Depending on the distance involved and the length of the line, one might have an anchor tied to one end while the other end might reach across the water and be secured on the far shore. In the latter case the line has an anchor at its center, holding it at a depth safe for boaters, water-skiers, and others.

To be checked periodically for fish, the trotline is "run" by the fisherman in a boat. Starting at one end of the line, the fisherman pulls it up hand over hand while the boat eases along. If a fish or a number of them have hooked themselves, usually they can be felt pulsating through the line. Regardless, hooks bare of bait are rebaited as they are seen, then dropped back into the water, later saving the time of doing it all over again. Two people in a boat make an easier job of this than one. The person in the bow can do the pulling of the line, help with boating fish, and move the boat progressively while the partner baits hooks before dropping the main line back to the lake.

A throw line is a short version of a trotline. One end is tied near shore, the opposite end is free but weighted, and the whole thing literally is thrown into the water. Throw lines are often used in rivers with currents making it difficult to secure and hold a line from bank to bank. Finally, bank pole and drop lines often used to catch channel catfish are made from bare essentials. These are commonly used on rivers rather than lakes. For a bank pole choose a sturdy but flexible sapling found on the shoreline. Cut it to a length of four or five feet, tie to one end a heavy line with a hook and sink the opposite end deep into the bank. Arrange the angle of the pole so the bait barely submerges. With other poles, baits might be set at different depths. Drop lines are tied to existing brushy limbs hanging over the water. Choose live, green branches, which won't snap easily. Obviously, there are more possibilities to choose from when a boat is used.

The secret of success with throw lines, bank poles, and drop lines is placement. In rivers the channel cat, which likes channels—hence its name, will be near flowing water above or below the riffles, near log-jams and deep holes. One ideal place to set lines is just below a shallow water shoal where the water plunges again to deeper areas. Another is above shoals. Jug and trotline fishermen should consider the same areas of lakes when they are available. Use the old river or creek channels and any creeks flowing into the lake. Areas with ledges and drop-offs to deep water often are productive. If there are stumps and trees standing in the lake, so much the better. Channel catfish are caught on these various lines set from a couple feet deep to 10 feet or so. If there has been a heavy rain and fresh water is flowing into the river or lake chances are excellent that channel cats will feed in the shallows. Rising water levels mean additional food is available to them. Usually, they don't let these opportunities pass.

This writer grew up fishing for channel cats on the Sangamon and Saltfork rivers of Central Illinois. Of the two the Sangamon was best, and it was a weekend ritual to spend from Friday evening through late Sunday on its banks. We invariably used three of the channel cat fishing tools mentioned here—bank lines, throw lines, and rods and reels.

First, the poles were cut for bank pole lines. After these were strategically placed the throw lines were baited and heaved into the current, then someplace conveniently between all this we settled down to man rods and reels propped up with forks of saplings stuck in the soft earth. Periodically throughout the nights we went up and down the bank checking lines, removing fish, and rebaiting hooks.

There is no better place to appreciate a big camp fire, the night sounds, and good companionship. There is also no better place to get your body all swelled up like a road-killed raccoon from mosquito bites, chiggers, and other terrible crawly things of the night. It wasn't that our motto foolishly leaned toward "Real men don't wear insect repellent." I would have sopped it on myself by gallons, had it been available and affordable. It wasn't, at least to us. Our money was better spent on gas getting to and from the Sangamon, and replacing lines and hooks lost in the river.

In retrospect, those were not the good old days of channel cat fishing. The river resources were all we had. These were few and miles apart. If the opportunities have changed for the better, the fish has not. The channel cat is the same we chased up and down the Sangamon River in Central Illinois. It follows the same patterns and daily routine, and it eats the same food it always has. In addition to those baits mentioned, this fish will be attracted to minnows live or dead. Shad and shiners are good ones for bait. Leeches are especially effective early in the summer season. So are chunks of raw bloody liver.

Because the average Illinois channel cat does not exceed two pounds, special tackle is not required. Obviously, line should be firm, perhaps 8 to 10 pound test is average for most spinning and spincast reels. With the reel's clutch or "drag" set properly to slip before the line breaks, very large channel catfish can be successfully handled with lines of these tests. Both are lines of common stoutness used by veteran trout fishermen accustomed to landing fish weighing upward of 10 pounds. This comparison is made because channel catfish and rainbow trout in many respects are remarkably similar. Within their respective habitats they are found in the same places, eat many of the same foods, and their skeletal structures are nearly identical, and when cleaned to the cooking stage they appear to be the same species.

The basic difference between these species is one of trout's being fooled more readily by artificials. Channel cats also hit lures, particularly when they spawn. Male catfish match the ferocity of largemouth black bass and nest-building bluegills. There is a spot on Crab Orchard Lake where Al Peithman caught so many channel catfish while casting for bass it was dubbed "catfish hole."

It was a channel cat that struck a plastic worm that demonstrated how one's blood can turn to ice water. Bill Bickers, of Champaign, is a friend of many years and a tournament fisherman well known to many Southern Illinois bass anglers. Bickers and I were together, using plastic worms for bass when a slight jiggle of the line indicated that a fish had picked up my lure. With a hardy jab upward, I set the hook in something unyielding.

Within two seconds this fish became so rough and rowdy it caused me to fantasize ownership of the elusive new world-record bass! I would be rich and famous, have at my beck and call tackle manufactures begging me to endorse their products. There would be thousands of rods and reels, tons of line and lures, dozens of boats and motors, all with my name handsomely engraved in solid gold. Profits from the tour alone would be worth millions, hauled to the bank in bales like hay. All this and more depended on what was at the end of the line, and there was no limit to this fish's stamina and fury.

Anxiety-filled minutes passed before the fish tired enough to be worked very carefully toward the surface, and for the first time Bickers and I caught a brief glimpse of its true identity. I felt like throwing up. Your little children do not want to know what I said. What I did was not a nice thing to do, either. With incalculable disgust, I heaved my tackle clattering to the bottom of the boat. The fish, of course, was securely hooked to the opposite end. Now it threatened to jerk the rod and reel overboard. Bickers bent down, grabbed up the rod and reel and shoved it toward me. "Here," he said nearly as bitterly disappointed. "Hurry up and land the damned thing so we can take turns stomping it to death."

This channel catfish did not meet a stomping end. Following the initial surge of regret that it was not the expected giant bass, cooler heads prevailed. In fact, Bickers and I finally came to a great admiration of this channel cat for taking us to the very brink of unimaginable excitement. The catfish was released unharmed. What did the channel cat weigh, you ask? Just six pounds hanging from a tackle box variety De-Liar scales. No bass this size I ever caught came close to matching this channel cat's swift line-straining runs and dogged determination.

Bullheads. Bullheads, worms, and muddy water go together like jam on buttered toast. This fish loves rising water conditions to bring it renewed sources of food. Illinois has all three species of bullheads—black, brown, and yellow—and of the three the black bullhead grows the largest. The average size in Illinois falls around one pound at the heaviest, so this is an eating fish rather than one destined for a wall plaque.

There are few people who have done much fishing at all in creeks, rivers, ponds, or lakes who have not caught bullheads. They are especially prime targets for live worms in early spring when rains swell waters to a roiled brown. Generally these are conditions not heavily favored by those who prefer the sunfish family members, but bullheads are excellent filler-inners until water conditions improve.

When a bullhead meets a worm it is hard to not stick around long enough to land the fish. They are incessant nibblers, pecking away at even the largest worm until they whittle it down to size, and when this remainder contains a hook it's a caught fish. For this reason numerous bullheads are caught on trotlines and similar multihook rigs even when fishermen are not in immediate attendance. This is one fish that can be completely ignored and still end up on a hook. When we talked about foods eaten by channel catfish we also mentioned bullhead foods, which are also the same as for all catfish discussed here. About the only difference between these catfish species in relation to the food they eat is the relative amount to the size of the species.

Also like channel catfish, bullheads spawn in spring, generally in June, and the male does most of the heavy work, selecting the nest site, guarding the eggs and fry. Eggs from an adult female number about 7,000 maximum for the black bullhead, up to about 13,000 for the brown species, and approximately 6,500 for the yellow variety. The life-span in Illinois for all three species is about four years, according to data provided by the Illinois DOC.

As an eating fish the bullhead is outstanding. Like other catfish, these are smooth-skinned without scales, so they should be skinned before eating. To prepare a catfish for skinning, remove fins and flippers while leaving the head intact, the better to grasp the fish. Make a cut in the skin just below the gills, pull the skin away from the flesh. Now, with pliers firmly grip the skin and pull it downward. It will peel away. Then remove the head and tail leaving only the firm meat to be cooked.

Catfish have skeletal structures which do not lend themselves to being easily filleted boneless. Generally catfish are cooked intact, then the meat is separated from bones at the time of eating. It is easy to do this by starting at the tail, and fingers are more efficient than forks. You will be forgiven, and may be applauded, even in the most sophisticated circles. Most people will be dying to do the same. Just probe around until the meat is raised from the skeleton, then the bony structure is easily pulled free and discarded. Now, you have slabs of steaklike fish instead of little fragments.

Flatheads. The flathead can get to be very large catfish; 35- to 40-pound specimens are common. For example, the Illinois record is 60 pounds 8 ounces. This minnow is overshadowed by the 91 pound 4 ounce world record. Rarely are these biggies caught on rod and reel, though it is obvious that these state and world records were or they would not be counted as such. For the most part, the average fisherman doesn't go prepared to hook one of these huge flatheads, so lines on average fishing tackle prove woefully inadequate when this occasionally happens. A 40-pound flathead eats for breakfast the size of fish most of us catch with rod and reel. Generally, it is left to those who use trotlines, throw lines, and drop lines hanging from branches to shorten the life expectancy of most flatheads. When this equipment fails to slow them down there is another, even more fascinating, method of taking these outsize catfish. This method, called "hogging," is legal in Illinois, though illegal in many other states. This is a pronounced form of insanity which can be very hazardous to one's health. If you don't drown with your arm crammed into the huge maw of a catfish, aren't bitten to death by a poisonous serpent, or disappear forever in some cavernous hole, you risk terminal skin shrivel from being soaked by river water.

A few years ago, Leonard Kuhnert, his brother Lee, and Roger Morgenstern, all of Pickneyville, gave cinemaphotographer John Kimsey and this writer a one-day crash course in state-of-the-art hogging on the Kaskaskia River. Leonard Kuhnert is a house-building contractor, Lee Kuhnert and Roger Morgenstern are coal miners, and all three belie the common idea that hogging, like baseball, is for young men. At this time Leonard was 58, his older brother two years his senior, and Morgenstern, who was considered the youngster of this group, was age 38.

Generally, flathead catfish spawn in June when river water levels are low and stable. They seek out large hollow logs and deep undercut banks, and cavities in log and brush jams in quiet water. In these places male and female flatheads get together to spawn. Amazingly enough, catfish in this posture do not seem to mind being touched or even fondled by the probing fingers of man. This allows hoggers to submerge and investigate logs and other bad places seeking docile catfish.

The Kuhnert brothers and Morgenstern investigated many places where more discriminating people, including this one, wouldn't dare venture to trust to a stick of dynamite, let alone probe barehanded. My head was filled with terrifying visions of snapping turtles with mouths like vicious bolt cutters and water moccasins so fat and powerful that a single hiss would blow me out of the water. Despite their nearly insurmountable handicap of towing along a couple very timid TV people, the Pinckneyville hoggers found and literally manhandled three large flatheads. Two fish came from the same submerged log.

The lightest of these catfish weighed 36 ponds, the heaviest 39 pounds. In order to find and overpower this flathead trio the hoggers were in the river seven hours. Are fish this bulky good to eat? Definitely yes, especially the flathead species. The Kuhnerts and Morgenstern say there is none better. Their neighbors and friends must agree because flathead steaks quickly disappear when this threesome hold their annual catfish cookout.

Flatheads have a life-span of from about 12 to 15 years, making them one of the longest lived of all fish species in Illinois. This same fish caught by commercial fishermen using nets have topped 115 pounds! The average weight of this fish in Illinois, however, is between 3 and 5 pounds, obviously in the juvenile to young adult stage. They begin to spawn when they reach a length of 15 to 18 inches. Fisheries biologists are uncertain how many eggs an adult female of the size caught that day by the Kuhnerts and Morgenstern would contain. No one has lived long enough to count them all.

Blue Catfish.   Perhaps the least known of the large catfish in Illinois is the blue. This is also the least common and the largest of the family. It is rare enough in Illinois that the state record, shared by two fishermen, at 65 pounds, has stood for 30 years. Both fish came from Alton Lake, a tributary of the Mississippi River. The world-record blue catfish weighed 97 pounds, and it was caught in the Missouri River in South Dakota in 1959. This is not to even mention, of course, the blue catfish occasionally caught in nets, fish which would dwarf these state and world records caught on rod and reel.

The greatest common mistake made when identifying channel catfish is to call them blue catfish. To be sure, some channel cats have a bluish cast, and both species have forked tails, yet the configurations of their tails are quite different. The blue catfish is primarily a species of big rivers while channel catfish are common to every size pond, lake, and river in the state. Even the most avid catfisherman could spend a lifetime at this pursuit and never lay eyes on a blue catfish. Blue catfish are rarely if ever deliberately stocked in Illinois waters. The few which happen to be in impoundments were there before the rivers were dammed.

Minnows and Suckers

Carp and Buffalo. Although the carp is in the minnow family and the buffalo is in the sucker family, they are lumped together here because of their similarities, which often lead to misidentification. First the carp. This is an example of good intentions gone awry. Originating in the Far East, the carp was stocked in Europe and the British Isles, then it was brought to the United States. While in many European nations it still is highly regarded as a sport and food fish, in North America it got completely out of control.

Maligned for years, the carp was originally supposed to be a welcome addition to our fisheries because it is vegetarian. It would not only help keep prolific weed growth in check but also provide food. Instead, what carp did was to cause untold damage to lakes, rivers, and ponds by their incessant roiling of the muddy waters, by literally wallowing like hogs in the shallows during the spawning of bass, bluegill, and crappie. This upheaval disrupts if not decimates nests and eggs of these fish.

At the same time bow fishermen take advantage of carp's highly visible, noisy spawning habits to shoot them in water often not more than two feet deep. Where there are a lot of spawning carp the archer doesn't have to hunt far to find targets. Chances are that carp will come to the bowman who stands quietly unmoving. The complete unwariness shown by carp spawning is a turnabout from their nature the rest of the year. Generally, this fish is spooky, nearly unapproachable in some clear-water lakes and ponds. This shyness is disregarded during the spawning season.

While armed with a fish arrow, I've stood in water 18 inches deep and had carp to five and six pounds, in the throes of spawning, slither right between my legs. They were too close to shoot. Carp are also taken by spearing, gigging, particularly when rivers and lakes flood and fish spread out to otherwise dry land. It's not uncommon for carp to be all over normally cultivated fields in flood stage right beside Route 13 between Carbondale and Carterville or a dozen or more places in Southern Illinois.

Say what you will about carp, this is a fish with strength and staying power to be reckoned with when it is caught on light tackle. Any fish that can reach a state-record 42 pounds and a world-record 55 ponds is a formidable species when trying to shake free of a hook. For those who deliberately fish for carp, baits made of vegetable matter such as doughballs generally are preferred.

One of the few positive things that can be said of carp is that they are available in just about every lake and sluggish river in the state. They are also caught by the ton each year by commercial fishermen using nets. These fishermen acquire special permits from state or federal agencies to take carp from designated lakes, and the fish are marketed.

As a food fish the carp had to overcome its unsightly appearance. To put it generously, this is not a handsome fish species. Once past this introductory repulsion, however, the meat of this fish is very good though bony. When left to the commercial fishing experts the carp is cleaned and filleted as boneless as it will ever get before being sold. The average fisherman doesn't have this expertise, so carp are cooked with most bones intact.

As a food fish buffalo is regarded as a cut above carp, generally bringing a higher market price for commercial fishermen.

For the average hook and line angler it is difficult to tell these species apart. The buffalo gets its name from the slight hump on its back, resembling that of the American bison. The Illinois state-record buffalo weighed 48 pounds, so this fish matches or even exceeds the carp in size. Again, they are not joined in the same family tree. The latter is a sucker while the carp is a minnow, as is the goldfish.

White Amur.   As recently as ten years ago few people knew what a white amur carp was. I'm sure there are some fisheries biologists who, today, wish they still didn't know what it was. There is concern that this fish will become a terrible repetition of the other carp. If it does, it has even greater potential for falling into disfavor with the American angler because of its sheer size. The white amur grows to be 100 pounds or more.

Native to the Amur River in Siberia and Manchuria, this carp found its way into Illinois probably through Arkansas, where they were imported for experimentation. They were cultivated in hatcheries for the specific purpose of stocking in ponds and lakes to rid them of excessive vegetation. Like other carp and other minnow family members, the white amur eats greenery by the ton. There are many lakes in the United States, particularly in the South, and notably in Florida, where water is threatened with literally being choked out of existence by unyielding vegetation. The white amur, or grass carp as it is also called, is viewed from some quarters as being the salvation of these waters.

From the outset, however, the Illinois Department of Conservation adopted a very cautious arms-length approach to the white amur. The DOC was moved to remind with no great subtleness the good folks of the state with flagging memories of the laws forbidding the importation of "exotic" fish species to the state. As all these warnings against stocking white amurs circulated throughout the state, a few Southern Illinois pond owners were busy watching their grass carp already at work gobbling up nasty weeds.

I visited one of these private ponds near Anna to fish for bluegill when the owner told me all about his white amur acquired from Arkansas. Were these fish doing what they were supposed to? No question about it. Like pigs they were rooting at the vegetation.

Shortly thereafter a white amur was reportedly caught in the Mississippi River, then another one in the Big Muddy River, still another one here, and one over there, etc. Today, the white amur is officially listed among the minnow family carp of Illinois. Might just as well be because it is here, though no one claims the credit for having wanted it. The best we can hope for is that the white amur doesn't get out of hand, and follow the same course as its predecessor. If it does, then, we've got a fish that is the size of a Shetland pony with a King Kong appetite.

Perch

Walleye. Walleye is a relative newcomer to Southern Illinois. In a few northern states and Canada, particularly Minnesota, Wisconsin, and Ontario, walleye is regarded as the reigning monarch of all food fish. But, the walleye is not a pike as it is commonly called. It is a perch, and like most freshwater perch its meat is firm and delicious. Many people are quick to swear there is none better.

This fish is native to northern cool to cold waters though in recent years it has been successfully stocked in many southern states including Tennessee. The world-record 25 pounder, in fact, came from Old Hickory Lake, Tennessee. Walleye has shown a remarkable adaptability to waters over the nation. The Columbia River bisecting Oregon and Washington is fast becoming renowned as one of the most spectacular walleye fisheries in North America. Here, walleye weighing 10 pounds or more are common. Recently, a new state-record 19 pounder was boated just below McNary Dam at Umatilla, Oregon, but on the Washington side of this great river. This gave the record to Washington.

Illinois walleye are not runts, either. They average up to about 4 pounds. The state record weighed 14 pounds. In Southern Illinois fish of 4 pounds are fully adult. This species does not reproduce naturally in this region; restocking is a continual process. The natural reproduction habitat for walleye is open windswept shorelines with gravel and sandy bottoms where weeds grow. The sticky eggs are broadcast and adhere to weeds, pebbles, and sand. Constant wave action is essential to keep the eggs oxygenated and developing. These structural ingredients generally are not incorporated in the makeup of Southern Illinois lakes.

Basically, walleye are minnow feeders though they also take all sorts of other food including worms. It was the live nightcrawler and walleye which gave rise to the development of the first plastic worm in the early 1950s. Because of their likeness to minnows, spinner baits and jigs are excellent lure types to fool this fish, and because of the walleye's penchant for worms the plastic variety takes its share of them.

No matter which bait, live or artificial, is used the angler must realize that walleye are deep-water fish. They shun bright sunny days, coming up only at dusk and night on bars, shoals, and ledges to feed. To my knowledge about the only place where the rule of weak light to darkness does not apply is in remote regions of North America, in Canada, where for decades walleye have stacked in holes like cordwood. There are so many of these fish the competition for food is incredible. They are on the prowl for food around the clock in shallow and deep water. But Southern Illinois fisheries are not the Canadian wilderness. And, as we have seen when an adult walleye is caught or dies, it is not immediately replaced by a hundred or more offspring.

Mark it down that walleye is a bad-weather fish. The most notable memories you'll ever have will form their beginning on days so blustery, chilly, and rainy that other fishermen won't consider being on the water. These unsettled days were made for walleye because the same sour weather patterns prevail in their natural northern climate habitat.

Think about it this way. Here is a fish that is accustomed to cold water conditions year-round, where in winter ice is so thick it safely holds the largest bulldozers and even airplanes. In spring and summer strong winds and high waves are a way of life, and one never goes on the lake even on the sunniest days without rain gear. Now, this same fish suddenly finds itself in Southern Illinois. Summer water temperatures of quiet, calm lakes are insufferably hot compared to those of far northern regions. Sunny, balmy days are the norm rather than the exception. It is no wonder that by spring and summer these fish become lethargic, staying deep in the coolest habitat, foraging away from it only at night when they see best.

February and March in Southern Illinois are like late April and May in the northern tier of the United States and Canada. Minnesota often has its best walleye fishing of the year in mid to late May. This means that the most productive times in Southern Illinois should be February and March, when it is still so cold that ice forms on rod guides.

By waiting until weather conditions are comfortable for human beings, we have waited too long. The peak of this fish's activity has passed, and the best we can hope for is to accidentally hook the occasional straggler. This is why it is common in Southern Illinois for a person to catch just one walleye, when down there in the same hole there might be a dozen or more. To be sure, this one fish may be a good one, fat and round bellied. At the same time, however, other equally fat and round bellied walleye are somewhere nearby. Walleye are a grouping if not a schooling species.

While the first rule of thumb is to put baits or lures deep enough, particularly during daylight hours, the second is that walleye are slow takers of baits and artificials. They do not chase and try to dissect their food. They take it hesitantly, gently. Lures in particular should be presented slowly, persistently, on and off the bottom. The exception to this rule is when lures are trolled. Groups of walleye, like most predator groups in competition, seem to have at least one individual that will not let an opportunity pass to snatch at a fast-moving lure.

Trolling lures is an excellent method to use in locating walleye, though it does not mean that additional fish will be caught from the same place by the same method. If it becomes clear that trolling is a failure, stop the boat and cast to this area. Allow lures to sink to the bottom, then manipulate them slowly up and down all the while bouncing off the bottom.

Another way to find this fish is to drift while bouncing a jig or spinner type lure or a jig with a live nightcrawler on its hook. Still another effective addition to the hook of an artificial is a live minnow. The minnow should be active and interested in its work. Generally, walleye are not enthralled by dead minnows.

When they feed, walleye are great travelers. About the time you think you have pinpointed the bonanza they are no longer there. To find more it's often necessary to search for them up and down the bar where the first was located.

More dependable are the size groups found in particular spots of any lake or river. A six-pound walleye, for example, will be associating with others of about equal size. There won't be many or any one pounders tagging at the heels of larger fish.

With teeth like a buzzing chain saw, walleye are as cannibalistic as any fish in the water. Big ones eat little ones. Despite these needle-sharp teeth it is the rare walleye that cuts a line with them. So no special leader is required between the lure and regular line. Walleye take lures like they do live baits, nipping at them. More often a bass will swallow a lure deeper in its gullet than will a walleye.

Nor is any special tackle required for this species. They are not spectacular fighters. While a large one may splash around at the surface, they don't leap from the lake with awe-inspiring antics. For many people ultralight spinning tackle offers the ultimate thrill in catching walleyes. The next greatest thrill is eating them. But, watch out for that mouthful of razor-sharp teeth! Grab one of these babies by the lip like a bass and you'll undergo an immediate and severe attitude adjustment.

Pike

Northern Pike. Completely different from the walleye is the northern pike. This one is a pike, the only one. All other fish species which resemble the pike are either pickerel or muskellunge. But, like walleye, this fish is native to the North, hence the name. Also, like walleye, pike do not generally reproduce naturally in Southern Illinois.

I added "generally" because Lake Kincaid holds the distinction of being the only downstate lake to ever produce a natural spawn of northern pike. This unusual occurrence took place as Kincaid was filling with water and pike had been stocked. Natural spawning habitat for this species is similar to that required by walleye. It happened that while Lake Kincaid filled, stocked northern pike were ready to spawn. They found in the weedy areas of shoreline compatible habitat for eggs and fry to survive. Though this reproduction was not spectacular, it was a fair one. And the only one ever brought off in Southern Illinois.

Once Lake Kincaid reached its current level all this natural spawning habitat had been inundated, so the initial success was strictly a one-shot deal for pike. They have not been known to find equal success since in Lake Kincaid. For a few years this population provided an excellent pike fishery. It was common for anglers to catch 8 to 10 pounders.

It was also common for fishermen to have spinner baits, plastic worms, and other artificial lures go thataway in a rush as they fished for bass. The sharp teeth of pike sawed through the toughest line faster than a blink. Pike can be rough customers. They hit lures with a dedicated vengeance, making certain that whatever it is doesn't escape. Often, lures are lodged so deep in their mouths that only long-nosed pliers or hook disgorgers are safe tools to use extracting them. This fish has teeth an alligator would envy. They make the walleye look like it gums its food to death. So, if you intend to fish purposefully for pike it is best to go prepared with a strong leader of at least six to eight inches tied between the lure and line.

As a rule these fish are loners skulking among the weeds and brush. When something edible comes near they pounce. This something can be any live thing from a frog to ducklings paddling overhead, which brings to mind the subject of noisy surface lures.

In July 1966, friends from Peoria and I flew by bush plane into Ontario's Lake Kukukus. In my tackle box were Lunker Lures, which I was anxious to try on pike. My companions—Dave Wolfe, publisher of *Handloader* and *Rifle* magazines; Bob Hinman, shotgun authority, also a book author; and Walter Schwarz, photographer—were getting the famous, fabulous introductory offer of this buzzbait.

As we operated on limited budgets, accommodations on this wilderness lake were about fifteenth class. The rickety old cabin had enough space between walls and windows through which to shoot a riot gun and never crack a pane. But fishing was absolutely superb. We ate walleye three and four times each day—walleye with eggs for breakfast, walleye with pork and beans for lunch, crispy golden brown walleye in bread sandwiches, and fat sandwiches made without bread, just walleye. The heaviest northern pike were caught on Lunker Lures. These fish were among the shallow weeds in early morning, waiting for something on which to jump, which is typical pike behavior. A hungry pike, which is most of the time, is a well-oiled feeding machine. A large one has no fear because it has no peer in its habitat.

Although the Illinois record pike weighed only 22 pounds 12 ounces, the world record went 55 pounds 15 ounces. Yet, a 20-pound northern pike of uniform physical solidity will measure right at 45 inches, nearly 4 feet long. Although the length of the Illinois state record fish is not listed, I'll bet that it didn't miss 45 inches by much one way or the other.

As water temperatures warm up, pike stay deeper, until in the heat of summer weeks it is hard to find them in the shallow areas. For this reason the best pike fishing is in early spring, late fall, and winter. In this case, in Southern Illinois, spring for pike can start in February or early March. Remember, they are accustomed by heredity to the same climatic water conditions as are walleye.

This fish will hit about any lure which wobbles, flashes, spins, or wiggles. In the North for many years the traditional best lures have been Dardevle Spoons of various sizes, with red and white the favored colors. The truth is that pike will just as quickly hit spoons of solid color, brass, or bronze, and any plug that looks like a large minnow. Plugs of various styles and sizes are excellent, especially those which dive to 10 feet or more.

Specific habitats within lakes favored by pike are strikingly similar to those favored by bass, the same places walleye and perhaps crappie will be found. These are the ledges, drop-offs, reefs, and channels near deep water. Pike like simply to come up and course into shallow areas with weeds or brush and lurk there in wait for an un-suspecting meal to swim within easy range. The lake which has pike and prominent land points plunging to the depths will have this spe-cies near these places. Islands, whether visible above the surface or submerged, are prime pike attractions.

Southern Illinois anglers have not been quick to generate great en-thusiasm for northern pike in their lakes, an attitude conforming to that of many other anglers across the nation. Some names given this fish in its native habitat of the North are not complimentary. It is called "snake" for one and "jackfish" for another. We must remem-ber, though, that northern pike and walleye generally share habi-tats, so the angler bent on filling a stringer with the ever-popular wall-eye views with disappointing disgust the occasional pike taking his offering.

In recent years, however, the pike has gotten a more favorable press than ever before. This is justified and deserving, since the pike is an excellent food fish. Skin it, get rid of the largest bones, and cook it like any other species. Its white meat is firm and flaky. On a number of occasions in Canada, pike provided some of the most delicious meals this writer has ever had for shore lunches.

As a fighter the pike is unpredictable. A 10 pounder or so will invari-ably let the angler know that a robust fish is on the line. But, I'm also convinced that many pike have no idea they are hooked. These fish are often hooked so easily it's disarming until they catch sight of the boat; then unexpected things happen in a flurry. Other pike will fight from the beginning jab of the barbed hook, and don't stop until they are completely exhausted. Then, at boatside they are easy to hoist aboard. Either way the angler is fully aware of having landed a tena-cious fighter.

Rainbow Trout

Catching a 5-pound rainbow trout, particularly in Illinois, is the equivalent of catching a 10-pound bass, a 1-pound bluegill, a 2-pound crappie, etcetera. It is not often done except in Lake Michigan. The rainbow is a highly respected game fish stocked in Devils Kitchen Lake in 1976 by biologists of the U.S. Fish and Wildlife Service. Of all lakes in Southern Illinois this was the place for rainbow trout to be.

Rainbows liked this lake and it liked them, which is rare in this state south of Lake Michigan. Rainbows do not survive just anywhere in Illinois.

They prefer clean, clear, cold water and Devils Kitchen has all this. It is cool enough with adequate oxygen at summer depths required by this species. Rainbows are classed as a cold-water fish species; they will tolerate temperatures at most to the mid-70s. They function best in temperatures between 45 and 65 degrees. Nature designed this fish to live in cool-water rivers and streams with ample oxygen dissolved in flowing water. Lake-dwelling rainbows go up or down seeking both compatible temperature and dissolved oxygen. The average Southern Illinois lake and the average river in Illinois does not have this essential makeup. This makes Devils Kitchen unique.

It has been a common practice for years annually to stock rainbow trout in a few small rivers and streams of northern Illinois, then open the season and let anglers have at them. Generally, these stockings are depleted with the majority fished out within days, which is just as well. Trout that survive angling pressure cannot escape the certain death of an incompatible environment. Thus, trout stocking by the Illinois DOC in these places is an ongoing annual exercise. Missouri carries on a similar stocking program once each year for its avid trout fishermen.

Very early spring, before bass, bluegill, and crappie are expected to be active, is an excellent time to fish for rainbows in Devils Kitchen. Late fall and early winter are equally good times to find them at relatively shallow depths. During summer weeks look for them deep, perhaps 25 feet or more, and use the tactics earlier outlined in the discussion about channel catfish.

Rainbow trout have a liking for earthy things such as worms, whole kernel corn, and Velveeta cheese. Of the many artificials used nationally and internationally for this fish, Mepps spinners, Rooster Tails, Beetle Spins and sinking Rapalas top the list of common lures available in Southern Illinois. Laying in a supply of these lures for fishing Devils Kitchen will not be a short-sighted investment if you intend to fish later elsewhere for rainbows. These same lures will catch this species anywhere in North America and anywhere in the world this fish is found. During a recent trip to Australia, we fished the Great Lake on the island state of Tasmania. Using Mepps and Rooster Tails, we caught both rainbows and brown trout weighing up to 5 pounds.

Not unexpectedly, the Illinois-record rainbow trout came from Lake Michigan, in May of 1984. By the time this is published, however, this record 24 pound 3 ounce fish could be history, replaced on the books by one larger. Lake Michigan is one of the most spectacular fisheries for trout and salmon this nation has ever had. The world-record rainbow came from Flaming Gorge Reservoir, Utah, in 1979. A comparison of its weight, 26 pounds 2 ounces, with the Illinois record clearly shows that Lake Michigan is fully capable of producing the next world record. Meanwhile, downstate anglers have the rainbows of Devils Kitchen to think about. It is a good thought, too.

Miscellaneous Species

Many fish species in Southern Illinois are about as well known as the African tsetse fly. For example, how many people lately have come up to you boasting that they caught a highfin carpsucker or a shorthead redhorse?

Yellow bass are common though few people correctly identify them. This fish is small, seldom exceeding 12 inches. It looks like a white bass with yellow undercarriage. To my knowledge nowhere do yellow compete with any other fish species for the favor of anglers.

The same applies to suckers and redhorse. The hog sucker (Yes, that's its name, really. Would I lie about something this important?) would not be recognized by one out of 10,000 fishermen. Perhaps this estimate is much too low.

Illinois also has, among other obscure species, mooneye and goldeye, drum, yellow perch (which is not so obscure) bowfin, gar, and sauger, plus a variety of seldom-recognized species in the sunfish family. Of these obscure species, the sauger, in the perch family, closely resembles the walleye, with the two often mistaken. Sauger is also an excellent food fish.

Although this may irritate smallmouth bass fishermen, the smallmouth bass is described in this section because it is not common to Southern Illinois. Experiments to introduce them have largely failed. The southern fringes of smallmouth habitats are located in central Illinois. Even here compatible waters for this species are few and far between. This is a shame, too, because smallmouths rate exceptionally high as a sport fish. They are great fighters, perhaps with more staying power than largemouth bass.

The spotted bass, also known as the Kentucky spotted bass, is another fish in Southern Illinois which, generally, is not recognized for what it is. A sunfish family member, spotted bass closely resembles the largemouth. Only the most experienced anglers who take note of the subtle differences can properly identify this species. Perhaps this is not good, either, because spotted bass is listed as a specific species with state and world records of its own.

The basic differences between the spotted and largemouth bass are: (1) spotted bass have teeth on the base of their tongues and largemouths do not; (2) when the mouth of the spotted bass is closed, the upper jaw does not extend behind the eye, while the jaw of the largemouth does; (3) below the lateral line extending from the gills to the tail of the spotted bass are numerous small spots, generally evenly distributed in rows, while largemouth bass do not have these rows of spots; (4) the two sections of the spotted bass' dorsal fin are joined, while these two sections on the back of largemouth bass are separated; and (5) spotted bass do not attain the size of largemouth bass. The state-record spotted bass weighed 6 pounds 12 ounces, and the world record went only 8 pounds 10 ounces.

We can, I think, also include here the rare species muskellunge, relative of the northern pike. This can get to be a vary large, toothsome fish. It won't be stretching the elasticity of the imaginary boundary of Southern Illinois to include here in that region a couple of lakes that have muskies, notably Lake Shelbyville and Hillsboro New City Lake. But, we won't lose our heads and go so far as to name also Clinton Lake in De Witt County as being geographically in Southern Illinois. The muskellunge is a fearsome creature, a miniature torpedo, unpredictable and totally unafraid of anything including boats occupied by fishermen.

Though I can't claim having met the hybrid variety of muskie, called the "tiger," there is story that bears repeating. A few years ago, Jack Ehresman, outdoor writer for the *Peoria Journal Star,* and I were fishing for crappie near Hayward, Wisconsin. This is muskie country where specimens topping 30 pounds are not uncommon. On display in one Hayward tavern are enough of these ugly-snouted fish to make the patron forget, temporarily, the objective for going in there.

Both of us were using ultralight spinning tackle and we had caught a half dozen or so crappie, when on his fragile four-pound test line, Ehresman hooked another one. The crappie was being routinely cranked up. It was barely two feet beneath the surface when suddenly there appeared an evil-looking dark figure rising beneath the struggling fish.

The first thing you notice when face to face with a live muskie is its blankly staring, menacing eyes. The eyes of this one were filled with a terrible fate for the crappie. The muskie moved as though gliding smoothly on ball bearings and grabbed the crappie. Then, a strange thing happened or failed to happen. As clearly as watching through a plate glass window, Ehresman and I saw the muskie with the crappie in its huge mouth do nothing at all. It just hovered right there, glaring up at us with hate-filled eyes.

The four-pound test line still holding the crappie was limp on the water now. Ehresman was helpless. With the crappie skewered by the clenched teeth of the muskie, there was nothing he could do but join me in looking on with amazement. For a full half hour the muskie controlled the situation with the crappie tightly clamped between its massive jaws. Occasionally it moved slowly, deliberately, just a few feet down and then up. Each time it did, Ehresman gave it the required length of line.

There was no question that the muskie was aware of the boat and us in it. It was also unquestionable that until the fish swallowed the crappie there was not a thread of hope that it could be sufficiently held by this light line. Even then, it would be asking for a miracle to land this muskie.

Finally, our patience at being held hostage by this belligerant creature defying us to do something about it wore to the snapping point. Ehresman gradually put pressure on the line. The muskie did little more than slightly raise its head. Then, as if to say, "Yes, I agree that it's time to end this nonsense," the muskie simply nodded. The line snapped. For a few seconds the fish hovered there, his cruel eyes leveled on us, then it turned and went away, the crappie still in its toothy jaws. Ironically, the reason Ehresman and I chose to fish for crappie that day was because the day before we had spent casting for muskies without a strike of any kind.

Compared to the army of people who spend every available minute fishing for more common species, however, very few deliberately set out to catch muskie in Illinois. The same can be said of freshwater drum. Indeed, this is a common species caught more by accident than by design. The Illinois-record drum, incidentally, came from Du

Quoin City Lake in 1960. This 35-pound fish was caught by Joe Rinella, of Mahomet.

Still another Illinois-record fish is the bowfin caught from Rend Lake by Charles R. Keller, of Sesser, in 1984. This one weighed 16 pounds 6 ounces. But I'm sure that Keller would be one of the first to agree that the average Illinois angler would be thoroughly baffled to identify his or her first bowfin. This also gives Keller the definite edge perhaps to establish another state record for this species.

Another miscellaneous species is the paddlefish, commonly called the "spoonbill catfish." But it is not a catfish, nor even related to this large family of familiar fishes. The paddlefish is, perhaps, one of the most ancient species in North America. Its exterior is held together by soft cartilage instead of by a skeleton made of bone. Paddlefish are vegetarians subsisting on plankton, so we not only don't catch them on baits and lures, but we also marvel at the tremendous size they attain. As one of the largest freshwater species, they grow to 200 pounds. Paddlefish are in the Ohio, Mississippi, and Illinois river systems and tributaries, though they are not ordinarily lake-dwelling fish.

Generally, they are caught in nets or by snagging during spawning runs as they scatter eggs over sandy or gravel river bottoms. Experienced snaggers know where and when to find them. They use large treble hooks on strong lines, bouncing these forcefully up and down until something solid is felt, and then the hooks are set.

In Illinois the average-size paddlefish doesn't exceed 5 pounds, which may be a generous estimate. Commonly caught, however, are fish weighing up to 30 pounds or more and 40 pounders are not uncommon. The Illinois state record stands at 52 pounds, caught (or snagged) from the Mississippi River in 1977. There is no world record for the paddlefish, probably because snagging is not an altogether acceptable way of establishing world records. And whether or not the paddlefish is classed as a game fish is an equally debated question.

Introduced Species: Good or Bad?

Based on the history of some wildlife introduced to the United States, it is justified for many fishermen to question the propriety of stocking what are commonly called cool-water species in Southern Illinois. These include walleye, northern pike, stripers, hybrid stripers, and muskies. Importation of the starling was a mistake. Introduction of the common carp, we learned too late, was downright ridiculous. The walking catfish, though not deliberately imported for stocking in public waters, still sends shivers rippling down the backs of authorities who had to deal with this misbegotten creature before it ate Miami. The jury is still out on the white amur carp. It will take years before we know whether the amur is friend or foe.

More recently the rusty crayfish instills fright in the hearts of fisheries authorities. Like the walking catfish of Florida, this one gets around, too, but it is believed that fishermen themselves are responsible for its distribution. It is said that in Wisconsin the rusty crayfish for the past dozen years or so has actually caused the displacement of game fish populations in some lakes. It plays havoc with crayfish populations, destroys natural vegetation, and in general disrupts game fish spawning processes.

Although the rusty crayfish is common to some areas of the Ohio River Valley, it is not commonly found in most rivers and lakes in Illinois, so it is being treated as an unwanted interloper, and perhaps a very dangerous introduction. Authorities believe that fishermen using this crayfish for bait dump the excess into the water at session's end. This is a common occurrence for both minnows and other live baits purchased by anglers at bait shops. Fisheries people feel that this is the source of the rusty crayfish's coming into Illinois. They also remind us again that dumping live bait into the water is illegal.

Then there was the duck-eating monster fish of Oregon as reported in the *Oregonian* newspaper in July 1985. The story dealt at great length with an unknown fish species suddenly discovered in a farm pond. The pond owner had caught a fish that weighed a tad over 11 pounds. He decided this fish was responsible for the steady disappearance of ducklings that had been on the pond. He also reportedly told the newspaper reporter that the fish had been dangerously aggressive. Before it was caught it had attacked him several times as he waded the pond while fishing. He claimed to have nasty teeth gashes in his waders to prove these attacks. At this point, I thought the article was a put-on, a hoax drummed up by the reporter on a slow day. But then he brought in and named the Oregon fisheries biologist who wasn't laughing about this "monster" fish discovered in his jurisdiction.

Before the biologist reached the site, however, the fish had been caught and cleaned. The news article reported the pond owner as saying that inside the fish's stomach was a fully adult mallard duck! It was a mallard drake, no less.

The upshot of this dangerously aggressive, people-attacking, duck-eating 11 pounder is that it was tentatively identified as a common channel catfish. I might give that channel cat a few of those hapless little ducklings, but I, and that catfish, would have a hard time swallowing the full-feathered mallard drake. Nonetheless, the very notion of an itinerant catfish in a place where it was not supposed to be evidently ruined that biologist's day. He was quoted as saying that the pond and others near it would have to be scoured squeaky clean to rid them of all channel cats which might be present.

In the Northwest, you must realize, salmon and trout are the preferred species, and, if there is a question about the well-being of these fish, the problem is resolved by ridding the waters of all suspect species, where and when this can be done. Ironically, channel catfish are commonly found in many areas of Oregon and Washington, and although they have their devoted anglers they are not a favorite species of these states' fish and game departments. Tradition favoring salmon and trout in the Northwest is just as strong as midwestern traditions leaning heavily toward catfish, bass, bluegill, crappie, and other spiny-rayed fish. It is also suggested that the Oregon pond owner gave an all-new meaning to the word incredible, and the person who wrote the catfish story was suffering an advanced case of ignorance. The channel cat is not your basic bad guy skulking through the night to taint unpolluted waters.

Conversely, there are good introductions, too, including the German brown trout, which is a highly respected game fish. The ringneck pheasant was an import from China to Oregon during the 1880s. The chukar partridge is another introduction that made good, and Texas, which is big on about everything, has its imports of exotic Asian and African wildlife.

The list of introductions that turned out to be terrible, however, is long enough to give anglers pause over the more recent cool-water species' mixing with traditional warm-water fish of Southern Illinois. The cool-water species previously discussed are predators with voracious appetites. They are fully capable of zipping through populations of bass, bluegill, and crappie with the speed and ease of a band saw cutting plywood. It requires a lot of food to satisfy a striped bass with a mouth the size of the bucket on a backhoe. Walleye and north-

Northern pike, which are not native to Southern Illinois, have been stocked annually in recent years in a number of waters. Since they cannot naturally reproduce in the region, there is no danger of overpopulation. (Photograph by the author)

Northern pike and muskies, introduced to Southern Illinois, are vigorous fighters. (Photograph by the author)

Not every angler will be interested in fishing for tiger muskies, but those who do will find this fish big and mean.

Rainbow trout caught with spinning gear. Medium to light tackle is ideal for fish species from bluegill to bass and from crappie to rainbow trout. (Photograph by the author)

The net, one of the oldest known fishing tools, is used to this day in modern sport fishing. (Photograph courtesy of Mercury Marine Corporation)

The camera catches the fish starting its high leap as the angler with spinning tackle holds on. Light lines and small lures are best with this kind of gear. (Photograph by the author)

Matthew Reid nets a bass located with the help of a depth finder—in this case a graphic model, which charts bottom structure. The boat is also equipped with a digital readout depth finder at the bow angler's seat. (Photograph by the author)

A collection of artificial lures that can be used to catch most species of game fish commonly fooled by artificials. (Photograph by the author)

The author with a nine-pound bass fooled by a seven-inch plastic worm. (Photograph by Steve Reid)

Fishermen gather before sunup to await the start of an early 1970s tournament. Note the lack of bass boats, which were just beginning to appear on the fishing scene. (Photograph by the author)

This four-man team of, *from left to right,* Paul Howerton, Don Gentry, Larry Switzer, and Bill McCabe, being congratulated by Dick Uptegraft, was consistently very successful at winning cash prizes and trophies in tournaments. (Photograph by the author)

enced was in Ontario near the Minnesota border when occasionally a northern pike would beat a smallmouth to the lure. We have outstanding crappie fishing in Wisconsin lakes where muskies also live. This list of coexistence could go on and on to include the bullhead catfish of Minnesota, a state renowned for this species.

The experience of Jack Ehresman and this writer with the crappie-stealing muskie in Wisconsin was rare to witness, though not unique to life beneath the water. The hooked crappie was struggling. It would have been obvious to the muskie that the troubled fish was an easy mark. Like all predators, the muskie did not let this opportunity pass. Some of the most effective artificial lures have been designed to simulate the spasms of injured minnows. Predators pick out these crippled fish from large schools. The Wisconsin muskie was doing no more than that when its jaw clamped down on the crappie hooked by Jack Ehresman. This does not mean that the lives of all crappie in this same lake are in jeopardy. Throughout Wisconsin basic muskie meals are comprised of yellow perch and large minnows. This same food pattern holds true for walleye and northerns over much of their natural range where yellow perch also live.

It appears that in Southern Illinois gizzard and threadfin shad fill the void where no small perch exist. In most lakes this is a definite plus. It helps to keep these prolific reproducers in check while also offering especially exciting fishing for walleye, northerns, tiger muskies, and stripers. Regarding the future, Mike Conlin, head of the Illinois DOC's Division of Fish and Wildlife, says it looks very bright. "Within the next five to ten years," Conlin says, "we hope to see Illinois anglers regularly catching muskie, striped bass, tiger muskie, hybrid stripers, and walleye. In the past, most of these species were not found in Illinois waters, in any significant number."

Illinois fisheries biologists have seen the beneficial impact of these same species introduced in other states, and they want to duplicate this success. Equally important is that it can be done when controlled. The built-in control is the failure of most cool-water species to reproduce naturally in Southern Illinois waters. This is very close to a guarantee that populations will not balloon unmanageably. Without reproduction, cool-water fish cannot threaten to displace desirable populations of indigenous species.

"We want our lakes to provide optimum fishing opportunity," Conlin says, adding there is no reason this can't be done. Furthermore, this is being done. The process was started some 10 years ago. More and more Illinois waters are becoming home for more of these well-traveled cool-water species. Striped bass and walleye in particular would have a hard time recalling their native lands or waters. Both are found all over the nation. As we have seen, the world-record walleye should come from the Columbia River. Ironically, it has been only within the past decade when the average Columbia River angler recognized a walleye when caught. It was considered a trash fish, and discarded with the same contempt given the undesirable squawfish of the Columbia. Illinois stands tall among states having cool-water fish species, since the state has an abundant variety. As Conlin said, the future looks good for the adaptability of these fish to Southern Illinois habitats. Now, all that fishermen have to do is to adapt to cool-water species.

4.

Tackle and Equipment

Tackle

It would not be an overstatement to say that for centuries there has been nothing new in basic fishing tackle. The fundamentals of fishing gear were in use before recorded time. Conversely it would not be an exaggeration, however, to say that for centuries fishing tackle has undergone a constant state of development and refinement.

For example, some of the first fishhooks were gorges, a crossbar made of stone or bone. These were tapered from the center to sharp points, and they had grooves around their centers where lines were attached. When a fish swallowed a baited gorge, a healthy pull on the line drove the point through the bait, and the gorge lodged crosswise in the fish's throat or mouth. If this rig and method sounds familiar, the principle of the gorge, is not different from that of the modern hook imbedded in the equally modern plastic worm. Ancient gorges of the type described have been discovered by archaeologists, who dated them as being from 10,000 to 30,000 years old. A gorge found in France was estimated by scientists to be at least 7,000 years old. This common ancient fishing tool has been found around the globe in the Artic, South Africa, the South Sea Islands, Switzerland, Scotland, and among artifacts of the oldest American Indian cultures.

Stone, horn, and shell hooks were being used by islanders of the South Pacific before these peoples were first visited by European explorers. Very sophisticated for their time stone, mother of pearl, and bone hooks were used by native Hawaiians and Solomon and Polynesian islanders when Captain James Cook sailed the Pacific in the 1700s.

Modern fishing tackle—that is, rod, reel, and line—was described in a book in 1651 by the Englishman Thomas Barker, who said that the "newest" principle was to incorporate the reel seated in the butt or handle section of the rod. In place of the word "reel," Barker used the term "wind," meaning that the angler had to wind the line back to a device that held it. But again, we find familiarity with the arrangement of the components of modern tackle that we take for granted.

The currently used spinning reel is the result of evolution, the refinement of line wrapped by hand around a stick or other cylindrical device. When the line was complete with the weight of hook and bait it could literally be swung and heaved away from the fisherman who simply pointed the line-holder in the direction the baited hook was to be thrown. In order to retrieve the line, the fisherman had to wind it by hand back to whatever held it. In many parts of the world this crude but effective method still is being used to cast a bait. When my son, Steve, with Bob Reeves, of Carbondale, and I fished Lake Yojoa in Honduras a few years ago we found native kids in rickety old wooden boats using the above-described method. The only modern twist was that lines were wrapped around pop bottles or beer cans.

No one really knows, of course, how far back in ancient times some type of hook and line was coupled, though a metal barbless hook was mentioned during the First Egyptian Dynasty, which would place it between 5,000 to 2,000 B.C.

The idea for mass-produced steel fishhooks came from China, though the Chinese do not take credit for this invention. They are credited, however, with using the first steel needles for sewing, and it was these needles that led to manufacturing steel fishhooks complete with the eye to thread the line. As Chinese-made needles traveled the trade routes, they were adopted and manufactured by other nations including England. Here, a needle maker took the steel device a step further, bent the shank, and added a barb; and by the late 1500s fishhooks were commonly produced by needle manufacturers.

The stamping machine introduced about 1825 took most of the hand labor out of making fishhooks as well as increasing production. The Mustad Company, of Oslo, Sweden, was founded in 1832, and it was this still-famous fishhook company which led the way in mass production using stamping machines to drill eyes in needles as well as fishhooks.

Today fishhooks are, of course, as common as morning coffee, and while once just a few hooks made entirely by hand were produced each day, now they are churned out so fast and in such volume it staggers the imagination. It would be nit-picking to try and find fault with the average quality of fishhook, except for one notable exception—brand new hooks out of the box are not as needle-sharp as they appear to be. Under a microscope they vividly reveal some blunt points which, generally, are insignificant until they fail to penetrate the jaw of a once-in-a-lifetime trophy fish. It is prudent to use a stone to sharpen every new fishhook, to touch up its point, and occasionally to resharpen as the hook or hooks is or are being used.

If there are two common causes for the loss of most fish, they are dull hooks combined with insufficient effort in setting the hooks deep enough. Novice anglers, especially, are normally timid about hook setting. Be aggressive and slam the hooks home with the intent of stretching the fish's body a few inches.

Lines

The first fishing lines were braided from everything from plant fibers to animal and human hair. The next logical step was to spin hair into lines. In the early 1800s lines were a combination of horsehair and silk. By 1900 silk had all but replaced the use of horsehair, and Italian silk was regarded as the best quality. China produced raw silk which was rough and considered unsuitable for the best fishing lines. Because of this roughness the Chinese called this line "grass line," though no grass was included.

The difference between silks of these two nations was a matter of boiling the materials. Raw silk has a gummy surface, and this gum had to be removed by boiling, making silk smooth and flexible while also reducing its weight. Just as Italian boiled silk of that period was considered the best for fishing lines, the very worst silk came from old clothing, dresses and other garments reworked and respun. These lines were the cheap lines of the day.

An inherent problem with silk lines made before the 1800s was limpness, resulting in a nearly unmanageable flexibility. The lines needed body, so experiments to stiffen them with grease or "dressing" were carried out as early as 1800. Fishing rods of this period were very long, up to 10 feet in length, and casts with limp lines were made with great difficulty. Some kind of dressing to stiffen lines and keep them afloat while reducing drag was required. It is not clear who was the first to use a greased line or where it was first used, but saturating lines with linseed oil was a common practice by both American and European manufacturers in the early 1800s. It was natural to call such lines "oiled."

American tackle makers were credited with the introduction of enameled lines, however. By the 1880s the United States was producing braided silk, waterproof lines for fly casting, which at that time was the most popular fishing tackle and method. Fishermen used these same lines on bait-casting reels, of course, though they were quick to fray and become weak from passing through line guides. Elisha Martin, of Rockville, Connecticut, was a bait caster who decided that he could make lines better than those available. He was in a perfect position to do this. As a silk dealer by vocation and a fisherman, Martin started braiding lines for himself and friends. This put Martin in the line-manufacturing business, where the Martin name endured until the company was sold in 1919 to the Horton Manufacturing Company.

Nylon replaced silk used in braided casting lines, then came monofilament, which today is used almost exclusively with casting, spinning, and spin cast reels. The early use of monofilament, however, goes back to leader material used between the fly line and fly, just as it still is with this fishing equipment. Monofilament and leaders contain the same type nylon.

Monofilament line will withstand an incredible amount of use and some abuse, but nothing of this kind is forever. Perhaps the two worst things that can happen to monofilament is overexposure to direct sunlight and dirt. Both significantly weaken monofilament, shortening its life-span. Being a very hard material, it is also subject to fraying and cracking, when it comes into repeated, strenuous contact with sharp or abrasive objects such as rocks and other snags. In order to prolong the life of monofilament, then, store it out of sunlight, keep it free of grit and dirt, and when you know or suspect the line has contacted cutting edges of snags inspect it often and carefully. Cut away this suspect section and retie the line and lure. Equally important, it is not a good idea to take the natural "stretch" from monofilament in order to straighten out the coils before it is used. This elasticity helps to prevent line breakage. Putting it another way, most of us have stretched a rubber band to its limits, then it snaps. Conversely, while a single rubber band retains its natural resiliency, it will last for many years.

Getting the hooks snagged and putting great pressure on monofilament in an attempt to free the hook or lure is another abuse of the line. Much of the line's resiliency is lost. Instead of pulling on the snagged line, it is best, when possible, to go toward the spot that causes the problem, then try to free the hook. If force must be used, less line will be damaged, and if it is necessary to break the line fewer feet will be lost.

The large amount of line we are able to stack on reels is, for the most part, totally unnecessary for average freshwater fishing purposes. The line-holding capacity of the average fishing reel, regardless of the style or brand name, will hold 200 yards of 10 to 12 pound test line. Obviously, the larger the line diameter the less yardage can be put on a given reel. Thinking about that, 200 yards is a pair of football fields placed end to end!

The average casting distance of lure or bait falls around 60 feet, and 75 feet or more is a lengthy one. Usually, it isn't necessary to make longer flings. Those record-setting casts across two canyons also get us into trouble; distance coupled with low line angle is susceptible to significantly more snagging than short casts. This means that, of this 200 yards of line on reels, we are using, at most, about 25 yards. Even giving or taking a few breaks here and there, and cutting away bad line at the end, few of us ever actually use more than 50 yards of line on any reel.

But the amount of line on a reel is very important to its overall function; all reels work better, more efficiently, when loaded to their respective capacities. It is, in fact, extremely difficult to make decent casts with too little line on a reel.

Still, we are left with one helluva lot of line on the reel which might just as well have disappeared into some black hole because it will not be seen again. This is why the word "backing" was coined. It was invented by fly fishermen who used fly lines of very sensible 20 to 25 yard lengths. Nonetheless, fishermen not only wanted some insurance incorporated in extra line footage, but, like casting reels, fly reels worked best when filled to the throat. So, fly fishermen put old lines, cheap lines, any lines on their reels first to fill up that empty gap, and they called this "backing."

Good line used for backing serves its purpose when the fly rodder expects to be fishing for species that will make sizzling runs farther than the fly line will accommodate. In this case a quality backing line is essential. A nonessential on the average fishing reel, however, is line that will not be used. Old line fills this void, saving the angler money. When new line is to be added to the reel, leave the old in place for backing and spool on only the amount you are certain will be functional.

The angler who intends to use a great deal of line will want to consider buying it in bulk rather than the ordinary 100 to 200 yard spools. The advantage, of course, is in using the exact amount of line needed at the time. Another consideration for installing new line on a reel is to take it to a sports shop that has a line-winding machine. These shops do the job efficiently, as they measure the amount of line installed, which is all you pay for. Machine-installed line can be especially important to owners of spinning and spin casting reels. This is in fact a good way to avoid the consequences of improperly installed line on these reels.

Spinning reels, in particular, tend to throw great gobs of line from spools soon after they have been reloaded. This frustration is caused by winding the new line directly from its spool to the reel as though one were reeling in a fish. Although this appears to be a perfectly logical way to install line, its the wrong way to do it. In order to eliminate trouble, the spinning line should be installed counterclockwise. As mentioned earlier, all reels are most efficient when line is loaded to spool capacity or slightly below it. Too much line, however, will have the opposite effect, particularly on spinning and spin casting models. When you come back to square one and face that terrible mess of excess line which just hurled itself into space, it's time to whip out a pocketknife.

Just as spinning was developed as a comfortable and much-needed alternative between fly casting and bait casting, spinning lines conform to a fitting pattern. Spinning reels are designed to use line weights of from about 2 pound test to about 15 pounds maximum. Lines heavier than 15 pounds defeat the purpose of spinning reels. Most freshwater model spinning and spin casting reels for fishing in Illinois and in the Midwest will give excellent service when used with lines of from 8 to 12 pound test. If a greater challenge is wanted, these reels also please the fishermen who use the ultralight models with line weights of from 2 to 6 pounds.

Lines for bait casting reels run the gamut from 8 pound test to more than 20 pounds. But even these sturdy reels begin to show a marked degree of inefficiency with line heavier than 25 pound test. Generally, lines testing 30 pounds or more are used for trolling freshwater lakes and rivers. To a great extent the weight and type of lure or bait to be cast determine which test line will do the best job. As a rule of thumb, the lighter the lure the smaller diameter and lighter the line should be. For example, it would be sufficiently disappointing to expect to cast with satisfaction a one-sixteenth-ounce lure tied to a 20 pound test line. To put it simply, the heavy line weight overwhelms the inertia generated by the one-sixteenth-ounce lure.

Another generalization about line weight selection is the clarity, or lack of it, of the water being fished. Most fish do see things in the water and many of them have excellent vision. All fish know all objects within their respective habitats just as people are aware of their home furnishings. Very clear water conditions, particularly during daylight hours, call for small-diameter lines. Cloudy to murky water is compatible with larger diameter lines. In this respect it is impossible for anyone to recommend which line weights are best under which water conditions. For example, let's compare the waters of three well-known lakes in Southern Illinois—Devils Kitchen, Lake of Egypt, and Crab Orchard. Of these, Devils Kitchen would have the clearest water year-round from the surface to just below the level of light penetration. Because of its clear water, the depth of light penetration would be greater than in the other two lakes. Generally, then, it would be significantly more important to use smaller diameter lines in Devils Kitchen than on Lake of Egypt or Crab Orchard. Again, one must make these on-site judgments according to water conditions of the particular lake. Just remember that if you can clearly see the bottom 10 feet down, fish can also see 10 feet up. The heavier the line, the more certain that fish can see it a couple of feet away.

On Barkley Lake in Kentucky, for example, there is a marina with a large minnow tank near the end of the dock, and directly beneath it a number of "pet" bass make their living. In every minnow tank there occasionally are a few bait fish that lack enthusiasm for the work they were created for, and these recalcitrants are culled out and dropped into the lake where they are hastily gulped by those patiently waiting bass. Generally, discarded minnows do not even strike the surface before a fish can be seen streaking from beneath the dock to accept this free meal, so we must conclude these bass see the minnows falling into the water. Also justified is the belief that bass are alerted to a potential shower of minnows falling their way by the vibrations of footsteps coming toward the minnow tank.

One day as I watched amused and no less amazed at the swiftness of these fish scurrying to intercept tossed minnows, the marina manager offered to demonstrate just how well these fish do see above the surface. Each sickly bait fish was thrown farther from the dock, and never in the same direction. Just a blink of an eye caused the observer to miss the entire fascinating scene. The speed of these bass was an incredible blur as each time a bass was there just as a minnow landed. This would tell us nothing, however, about the vision of bass if they had learned to just stay out there where they expected minnows to land. This was not the case. To the contrary, following each thrown minnow, bass retired to hiding in the deep shadows beneath the dock where they waited for the next food to be served.

To return to lines, in recent years extensive research efforts have gone into making lines as "invisible" beneath the surface as possible. Manufacturers have largely succeeded in removing a great deal of visibility from lines, which helps to make modern lines the most efficient the fishing world has ever had available. This is especially true when clear water is being fished.

Finally, the test strength or poundage of a particular line is measured by its breaking point. For example, presumably, it takes 10 pounds of stress to break a 10 pound test line. This is not necessarily uniform, however, with all lines. Breakage can, and often does, occur on either side of the designated test strength of individual lines. Fortunately, lines usually are a little stronger than the numbers on the spools indicate. Manufacturers measure line tests by their dry strength. There is a difference between wet and dry strength of all lines; they lose some of their strength when wet. For this reason, as a general rule, the true breaking point of dry line is greater than indicated by the numbers, which compensates for the loss when it is wet. So, when our example 10 pound test line is bone dry it is common for it to withstand a stress of 12 pounds or more.

But it's a mistake to rely on every line being stronger than the test marked on the spool. In rare cases a line will not measure up to its designated breaking point. The buyer has no control over the age of the line; how and where it was stored (in shaded spots or in direct sunlight streaming through a plate glass window); or, with some bargain lines without the name of a known manufacturer, what quality of line it happens to be.

This brings us to the fact that throughout the world only a handful of manufacturers actually produce all monofilament, which is in turn marked with numerous brand names by tackle companies that sell line. A spool stamped Brand X doesn't necessarily mean it was manufactured in the plant of Brand X.

Not long ago I visited a tackle company that is regarded as one of the largest of its kind in the nation, and they had recently reached out into the line market. It was the reverse of making mountains out of molehills as their line department made little spools of line from incredibly large bulk rolls of monofilament purchased from an eastern manufacturer. Individual companies who stamp their names on lines and market them do have control over test strength if and when this research is carried out in their own plants.

This brings us full circle back to those bargain lines which are not labeled with the names of well-known tackle companies. Chances are that the line is good material and has the test strength indicated, though the buyer has no inkling what, if any, quality control preceeded marketing these lines.

Reels

As mentioned earlier, the first record of a "wind" or reel was in a book written by Thomas Barker published in 1651. A revised edition of this book published in 1657 included an illustration of this reel. Barker described this mechanism as a "wind to turn with a barrel to gather line, and loose it at the angler's pleasure." The reel, according to Barker, was seated in a hole in the rod handle. Until that time in fishing history common equipment consisted of a very long, stout wooden pole, braided line, and hook. This combination is still used in what we commonly know as cane pole fishing. Only the poles have changed.

Most poles were indeed poles and not flexible rods, and for good reason. Before the invention of the reel, fishermen commonly followed a procedure that would puzzle today's anglers. When a fish was too large and powerful to land, fishermen simply threw the pole into the water! The thick wooden pole floated, of course, which helped eventually to tire the fish. The fisherman followed the floating pole and then landed the exhausted fish. If this ancient method suggests a contemporary fishing practice, it would be jugging for catfish. The systems are similar, though plastic gallon jugs have replaced wooden poles.

Although Barker was first to write about the use of a reel, both he and history neglected to tell us who invented it. There is not a doubt, however, about who invented the first "multiplying" reel for bait casting or where the person lived. George Snyder, of Kentucky, was a watchmaker of the early 1800s who lamented the fact that the single-action reels of his day generally had bad characteristics when large bass were being handled. Single-action reels were then and are now of the fly-reel type from which line was and is pulled by hand. So Snyder set about building a reel with a spool that would revolve, paying out line with the cast, and winding line back to the spool when a handle was used to turn the spool. As a watchmaker, Snyder had the skill to do the job, and as president of an area fishing club he had companions eager to own one of his reels. From about 1810, Snyder continued to build reels for a number of years, though it remains a mystery why he did not launch into commercial production. It took another enterprising Kentucky watchmaker to do this.

B. F. Meek had a shop in Frankfort, Kentucky, when around 1830 he was prevailed upon to replace a coveted Snyder reel that had been lost by its distressed owner. Evidently the reel Meek made was as good as or even superior to the original Snyder reel. Meek then made reels only part-time until about 10 years later when his brother came into the business, when they divided their efforts between making reels and watches. Now bait casters had a superior reel. Compared to the old-style single-action contraptions, the Meek reel performed magnificently. Others thought so too. Manufacturing rights to the Meek reel were secured by the Horton Company, of Bristol, Conn., where until 1941 the reel was produced under the Meek brand name, with production being stopped by the war.

World War II also had a retarding effect on the acceptance in America of the spinning reel system. Spinning reels came across the Atlantic from England, where in the early 1900s this was common fishing tackle. At this time, however, American anglers virtually ignored the spinning system. It is said that in the 1930s when a few spinning outfits did find their way to American tackle dealers they went unnoticed and then were put away with memories of them dulled by time. For example, how many of us even remember the Mastereel made in America by Bache Brown prior to 1941, when the war stopped production? Following the war, in 1946, the Mastereel revived. This was the first spinning reel brand of which this writer has a recollection. About the same time the Mastereel awakened from its forced slumber the Humphreys reel made its way from Denver to the U.S. fishing market. And for all intents and purposes, spinning, a method steeped in antiquity, finally wrenched free of its obscurity in the United States.

Once discovered, spinning held an immediate attraction because of its operational simplicity. Because the spool holding the line doesn't revolve, doesn't move at all when the cast is made, this reel is virtually free of all troublesome backlashes. While this alone was compelling reason for anglers to try spinning, they also found that for the first time, with spinning tackle, they could cast very light lures and baits.

The multiplying bait casting reels were at their best with the use of relatively heavy lures or bait weighing a quarter ounce or more, and their performance shone with lures weighing five-eighths of an ounce or so. By attaching a plastic bubble to the spinning line above the lure, these reels and rods handled sufficiently even the lightest of flies, converting this versatile outfit into a passable fly rod. Spinning tackle does all this because its mechanism generates so little friction. The reel spool is stationary, the rod is long and limber, and on it are guides of larger diameter than those used on bait-casting rods. There is so little to interfere with the energy of casting that the lightest lures and baits are used with satisfaction.

As we have seen, monofilament line made of solid nylon came on the scene about the same time spinning arrived. This combination was unquestionably the death knell of the old-style multiplying bait-casting reels and the braided silk lines commonly used with them that were so commonly made through the 1950s and into the 1960s. The prevailing attitude of that time was why mess around with archaic equipment with its frequent and irritating backlashes and lines that neutralize casting effectiveness when spinning tackle was a lot more versatile?

There is a marked difference between the mechanisms of the original multiplying casting reels and what today we refer to as "free spool" casting reels. First, gears of the former models were constantly engaged with the spool and reel handle. When one of them was set into motion all of them worked. By design, then, when a cast was made the handle started whirling violently backward! Secondly, these reels contained no brake or stop or anything else which would prevent their handles or spools from slashing rearward as the hook was set in a fish. It was essential to grasp the handle and hang on. The inflicted pain at being surprised by a fish hitting the bait was called getting your knuckles busted. But it did serve to keep you more alert. Finally, all those gears and handle and spool clammering around together gave a whole new meaning to the word friction. This sluggishness, coupled with the fact that the fisherman had to apply constant thumb pressure to the spooled line, made these reels vulnerable to the many significant improvements incorporated in the newly introduced free spool casting models. The outdated multiplying reels went belly up in the late 1960s.

Nevertheless, in isolated pockets of the nation tradition was not quickly displaced by fancy new fishing tackle. Southern Illinois was one of those places. When, in the final month of 1964, I moved from Champaign-Urbana to Carbondale, one of the first fishermen I met was Bill Harkins. As manager of the Play Port Marina on Crab Orchard Lake, Harkins had his finger on the pulse of everything to do with fishing in and around this area. He introduced me to a lot of fishermen, and I was surprised to learn that so many of them clung tenaciously to old-style bait-casting reels.

Harkins used one as did Jim Aaron, Hack Jackson, Bill McCabe, and John "Gino" Swetz among a score of others who were regarded as an elite cadre of bass fishermen. To a man their favorite reel was the venerable Shakespeare President, used with a five-foot six-inch rod. This reel was the very best produced by the Shakespeare Company. In the heyday of this style of multiplying reel, the Shakespeare President and the Pflueger Supreme shared the top of the heap. They were the ultimate goal, the enveloping dream for every young angler to own. When you could proudly lay claim to ownership of this property you had arrived as a fisherman. But not until. Southern Illinois held its share of proud anglers.

One day Harkins arranged a meeting with Jim Aaron, of Marion, and a few days later Aaron and I fished Crab Orchard. At the outset, Aaron looked askance at my tackle. It was one of the latest ABU Garcia free spool bait casting reels on a six foot glass rod, to which my host gave a fleeting glance of displeasure. He remained discreetly silent about it, however, for awhile. Aaron's equipment was the aforementioned Shakespeare President with a rod of about five and a half feet.

It was one of those delightful April days which God created especially for fishermen. He fashioned this day particularly for fishermen who found immeasurable thrills in using surface lures. Not a ripple of water was stirred by even the most vagrant breeze as Aaron guided the flat-bottomed johnboat into the neck of a wide cove. He then shut off the motor and bent over his tackle box. My eyes scanned this promising place.

Around this horseshoe-shaped cove weed beds grew from the shoreline to from five feet to about fifteen feet into the lake. In places the weeds formed a thick carpet on the surface. There were also many spots where the weeds gave way to open pockets of water where, with great anticipation, a lure could be cast right to the uncluttered shoreline, then retrieved. These splotches of relative openness were important to me because I did not have with me surface lures which would penetrate the maze of vegetation without becoming snagged with every cast.

Aaron solved this puzzle for me by taking from his tackle box the most ungainly conglomeration of metal, wire, hair, and hook I had ever seen. "Here," he said handing a lure to me. "Let's try these." The lure had an aluminum propeller so large that with a small motor it would provide cheap air transportation.

"What do you call this thing?" I said, flipping the propeller into motion with a finger.

"It's a Lunker Lure, made right here in Marion by a friend of mine, Hack Jackson."

Then Aaron tied a Lunker Lure to his line as I followed suit with mine, still wondering how to use this strange thing. My bewilderment must have shown. "It's a surface lure," Aaron said. "The minute it hits the water start it moving. Keep it on top and reel just fast enough for it to churn the water."

As he demonstrated the lure, I was amazed at how it was cast directly into or past the weeds, then retrieved right through or over them without becoming hopelessly snagged as most surface lures would be. The slurping noise made by the Lunker Lure's propeller coupled with the widening V-shaped wake behind it was positively mesmerizing! If this terribly ugly apparatus held just half the appeal for bass as it did for me, we would, undoubtedly, quickly fill this little boat with fish. All of a sudden this apparently simple casting effort took on all of the aspects of a duel to the death. Although Aaron made casting his lure look easy, mine had a penchant for sinking. Before I could retrieve it fast enough it was wallowing beneath the surface just before clinging tight to unrelenting weeds.

Following the fourth time Aaron had obligingly sculled the boat to the shoreline so I could dislodge my lure, I sensed that he was about to tell me something. His face was somber. "Maybe it's your tackle," he said. "I've never seen a reel like that. What is it?" I told him about the reel. The basic difference between his and mine was that the Garcia free spool disengaged from all those interior gears when the cast was in motion, and it had all kinds of fancy adjustments for spool tension, line size, and lure weights. When he shook his head slightly, I also sensed that he wasn't impressed. "Well, then," he said, "it could be that your rod is too long."

I let that pass without comment. My problem with the Lunker Lure was one of timing, and not with the tackle. But the lure was making me feel as helpless as a beached whale, so it would have to be mastered quickly. Time for caution had passed or Aaron would be justified in using the new kid on the block for a boat anchor. From that moment on, I scorched the air with sizzling casts and brought the Lunker Lure back while it made tracing rhythmical little sounds on the surface. That morning we caught three bass. From that introduction to this lure, I became a devoted user of it and one of its highly vocal advocates.

It would be a few years, though, before Jim Aaron and other hardcore bassing men of Southern Illinois would reluctantly give up their prized reels in favor of the newer free spools. In fact, Bill McCabe, also of Marion, was awarded a new Shakespeare President for placing in a tournament in 1968. This was one of the last of this reel type I ever saw brand new in Southern Illinois. I'm not altogether certain whether McCabe ever used this reel because he, like nearly everyone, was making the transition to the free spools imported from Sweden. That "red reel," the Ambassador 5000 marketed by ABU Garcia, would become the undisputed monarch of bait casting reels of the early 1970s.

Meanwhile, renowned bass fishermen such as Al Peithman, of Carbondale, already had recognized in spinning tackle the qualities they couldn't hope to match with conventional bait casting equipment. Peithman was one of the early users of spinning rods and reels, particularly for summer fishing in medium to deep water holes. Deep water was Peithman's forte, and his reputation for catching bass in hot summer weeks was widespread. For years before I moved to Carbondale, I knew about Al Peithman, knew about his often incredible catches of bass, about the equipment he used to ferret heavy fish from their offshore habitats.

Anyone who consistently catches so many fish during weeks when so few others make the attempt also makes good newspaper copy. Peithman filled a lot of space in newspaper releases filed from the Southern Illinois University News Service. This office on the Carbondale campus was headed by the late Bill Lyons, himself an avid fisherman, and the information compiled and written by his associate, Pete Brown (who heads this office now) was mailed to newspapers all over the state.

As the outdoor writer for the *News Gazette,* of Champaign-Urbana, I eagerly looked forward, like a starry-eyed fan, to ongoing information about Peithman. It was natural then, when I moved to Southern Illinois, Peithman and I would meet. I met a giant of a man six feet three inches tall and nearly 250 pounds with the strength to crank a spinning reel faster than anyone I had ever seen. His favorite tackle was a Mitchell 302 light saltwater reel and at the end of the string was a Bomber, usually an all-white color with a single black wiggly line down each side. Peithman bought these lures by the dozens.

The Mitchell 302 had a greater line capacity than the smaller Mitchell 300 used by the average freshwater angler. So, with this reel on a seven-foot rod, Peithman could shoot the 400 and 500 series Bombers like rifle bullets and nearly as far.

This reel not only had a fast retrieve speed but it also plunged the Bomber to its deepest potential. The lure was attracted to snags like nails to a magnet, and, with it moving so swiftly, its hooks skewered stumps. When a Peithman Bomber hung on an immovable object, Peithman would break or cut the line, leaving the lure stuck to the snag. A hastily tied new lure put him back in business without moving the boat. Obviously, this expeditious practice required one helluva lot of line on the spool, not to mention a never-ending supply of lures.

When Peithman called the Bomber Bait Company, they listened, gleefully.

What made Al Peithman unique or nearly so among fishermen of the 1950s and '60s was that his fishing tackle for Southern Illinois waters was not only unconventional, but few others knew how or where to catch midsummer bass. Ironically, Peithman was totally uninterested in going to the lakes before June!

Following the wide acceptance of spinning tackle in the United States another form called spin casting swept across the land. Although both incorporated the same principle of nonrevolving line spools, spin casting reels were and are physically different in a number of interesting ways. First, spin casting reels are completely enclosed in a housing; spinning reels are open, the line visible at all times. Secondly, spin casting reels are mounted on top the rod while spinning reels fit beneath the handle. Finally, in order to activate the spin casting reel all that's necessary is to push a handy button situated in a natural position right under the fisherman's thumb.

Conversely, the spinning technique requires more steps. First, the line is picked up and held manually by the index finger, then the line bale to release the line is opened with the other hand. The line must be held firmly by the finger while the backcast is in motion, then released at the right time on the forward cast. It isn't as complicated as it may appear to be. The trick to mastering the spinning reel is in timing the release of the line with the finger. Chances are, though, the first couple of casts made by the novice will end up rather surprisingly behind him or her, or they will go straight up in the air. Don't fret about this. It happens to nearly everyone, including skilled casters, who use spinning reels for the first time.

Usually, this is not the case when breaking in with a spin casting reel and rod. Just push the button and fling, which is one reason why this combination vaulted to instant popularity and still holds an incredible share of the fishing tackle market. As the name implies, spin casting is a compromise between spinning and bait casting tackle, and so being it includes the best features of both. Like bait casting rod structure.

If there is a single source who very early in the game was responsible for putting inexpensive spin casting equipment in the hands of literally millions of fishermen, it was the Zebco Company. In the 1960s for less than five bucks the angler could joyfully leave the sporting goods store with a complete Zebco outfit—reel, rod and line. These tough little reels were so inexpensive that when they went bonkers, if they did, likely as not they were tossed aside and a new one purchased.

The final important difference between spin casting and spinning reels is that the former always comes equipped with factory installed line; spinning reels do not. Nevertheless, extra spools of line can be purchased for both.

A personal recommendation for the neophyte is to begin with the easy-to-use spin casting tackle. It is simplicity personified, and starting with it may eliminate screams and loud ugly noises so common when the beginner uses other tackle types. Spin casting is a good choice for the introduction of youngsters to fishing. If you find that their early determination has switched to absolute indifference, the cost of investment in this tackle is less bothersome.

The Garcia Ambassador 5000 became the standard by which all free spool reels were judged. This reel adorned the casting rods of all serious bassing men. For a number of years it held this enviable position until the same company introduced a new, improved, version with the same basic features, but with a notable difference: This new model also had a shimmering black coat. It was, however, unmistakably Garcia Ambassador. Just how good were these reels and other imports? They were the very best imaginable.

If Jim Aaron reads this he will find some ironic pleasure in knowing that my reels still are the same as those introduced in the 1960s. Despite the mind-boggling array of improved, refined Mags, Ultra Mags, Bantam Pro Mags, Magforces, and Procasters not a single example of them do I own, or for that matter even have a burning desire to own. The point is that I don't need new reels. All of mine perform admirably as they have for more than 20 years. Need more be said about quality? Occasionally over the years, when the rare repair was necessary to one of these reels, I didn't fix it myself, following the first tragic error in my effort to discover what's inside one of these suckers. I couldn't slam the cover fast enough to prevent an explosion of irretrievable, minuscule parts and springs. After that, I shipped reels to people who are a lot smarter than I am about repairs.

Rods

In the late 1940s glass made inroads on bamboo and steel fishing rods. Bamboo rods were also commonly called "Tonkin cane," named for the province of Indochina where the best bamboo for rods was found. Today, custom-made by special-order split bamboo rods are about as expensive as the upkeep of a daughter in high school. Glass incorporated closely the action of bamboo, yet it was more rugged, withstanding the terrible violence some of us heap upon our fishing tackle. Importantly, we could also afford to own glass rods, which, generally, were lighter than the steel rods of the day. Tubular glass rods became so popular during the 1950s that 10 years later it was extremely rare, like passing a Ford Edsel, to see one made of other material.

The next giant step in rods was the introduction in the 1970s of graphite. These rods were lighter than glass, smaller in diameter, and far superior to glass generally. The prices of graphite rods were high, however, with the price of the average rod being around $60! It cost less than that to bring our first-born son into this world. The price of graphite is the one thing which has not toppled glass rods from the throne of popularity among the weekend fishing army. Quality graphite still costs a bundle.

Quality is the key word here. Not all graphite rods are quality and not all graphite rods are all graphite. To the contrary, commonly incorporated with this material is plain old glass, the same glass which is used in less expensive fishing rods. As it stands now, as this is written, there is nothing to prevent manufacturers from making rods with 10 percent graphite and 90 percent glass and advertising them as "graphite." And we have absolutely no way of knowing how much of which material is in a particular rod we are considering buying. As a case in point, studies have been made and researchers have found that many rods contained more glass than graphite. A few contained a heavy percentage of glass. Yet these, too, were advertised as graphite rods.

This strikes me as being not altogether right. It strikes some people in the tackle industry the same way. The Berkley Company instigated a move for the industry to clearly mark all rods with content of materials, then let quality stand on its own. Even if this comes about it does not mean, however, that glass will no longer be used in making graphite rods. It does mean that we will, at least, be aware of the percentages of respective materials in each rod.

Not too many years ago buying a fly line to match a particular rod action was an equally chancy business. There was no standard of weight and diameter measurement throughout the industry. Each line maker produced its product according to its own secret method, at the frustrating expense of the befuddled fisherman. Let's say, for example, that you own an eight-foot medium-action fly rod of Brand X that the manufacturer claimed performed its best with C-level line for all-purpose casting. The trouble with this was that rod makers didn't produce lines, so they were assuming, guessing, and perhaps praying a little that they were right. Too many times they guessed wrong, particularly when the fly rod owner shopped the various brand lines. It was not only possible but probable that the variances between C-level lines forced the bewildered fly rod owner to buy a number of them before discovering one which performed with satisfaction. Finally, however, rod and line makers discovered they did, after all, share a mutual interest. The result was the first uniform scale of line manufacturing measurements and weights used by line makers.

Now all fly lines go by a simple numbering system, and fly rods come fresh from factories with the recommended number (size) line best suited to its action. Fly rods, in particular, are very finicky about such things. This is the only fishing tackle with which we cast the line and not the lure. The fly or popper alone does not have enough weight to be hurled into space like heavier casting lures. For this reason it is essential to pleasurable moments with the fly rod for the fisherman to strike the necessary balance between rod action and line. When it is thrown out of kilter by using the wrong size line, casting becomes a grim experience. You'll want to toss the whole thing in the pond and go quickly to find the ingredients for a two-day hangover.

Nevertheless, fly fishing is one of the oldest methods of sport fishing, brought to America from England. Even today the English favor the fly rod over other types of tackle. Bait casting is purely American, invented and developed here. It has not had a sweeping success around the world. While in Australia, and particularly on the island state of Tasmania, we found fly fishermen outnumbered spinning casters ten to one. Tasmanians don't even talk about bait casting for freshwater fishing. Bring up this subject and they fix you with a hard stare sufficiently grim to frighten Frankenstein.

Generally, the proper length, action, and weight of fly rod is chosen for the type of fishing it will be used for. Short, lightweight rods up to seven feet are ideal for fishing confined casting quarters and for bluegill and crappie. These same rods, however, would fall short of handling larger, heavier flies and poppers used for bass fishing. Bass action rods are eight to nine feet long, with the backbone to whip out sturdy flies, streamers, and poppers of a size attractive to bass. Putting it another way, the larger the fish species being cast to the longer and heavier the rod and its line should be.

Another generality is that fly rods of from eight to eight and a half feet long with medium to heavy actions serve well as all-purpose fishing tools for Southern Illinois waters and species. With such a fly rod the angler can go about anywhere in the nation, including Alaska, without being clawed by the raw fear of having tackle smashed to pieces. Heavyweight king salmon in Alaskan rivers, though, should be approached with due caution by using sturdier fly rods.

As pointed out, there is a great difference between the physical structures of bait casting and spinning rods and some difference between bait casting and spin casting rods. We must remember, too, that spinning was developed as a compromise between bait casting and fly fishing, so these rods reflect this basic idea. But for now we'll take them in the order of their respective appearances on the North American fishing scene.

Modern rods for bait and lure casting, particularly rods made of graphite and the newer boron are relatively short, ranging from five feet long to about six feet, and the average is five and a half feet. The theory is that a short rod gives greater control over precise casting of lures. This is especially true when casts are short-distance, such as when fishermen are cruising near shorelines and aiming lures with pinpoint precision.

Another reason for relatively short casting rods is the materials used to make them. One appeal of graphite and boron, another rod material, is lightness; and weight is reduced by making rods small diameter compared to those of glass, but without sacrificing strength even in rods a little shorter than those of glass. Although glass rods are somewhat heavier than graphite, this weight isn't at all prohibitive or even significantly noticeable until a rod of each material is compared in each hand.

Of jolting significance are the price gaps among quality boron, graphite, and glass. On this scale boron is most expensive, graphite expensive, and glass the least expensive. And please don't expect me to explain boron. I was just getting used to the difference between glass and graphite when this new stuff surfaced.

All bait casting rods have the same basic features—a handle with a comfortable grip, a slot in this handle for a top mounted reel, and line guides conveniently spaced along the rod. The tip is the last of these guides. Referring to quality again, on some of the best-made rods there are at least six guides including the tip on a five-foot six-inch rod, and these guides will be of a hard material, such as silicon carbide or something similar, which prevents wear from the line.

Spinning rods, on the other hand, range in length from five feet six inches to more than seven feet, with the longer rods preferred for casting the lightest lures and baits. The reel is mounted below the handle, and in line with the reel are the guides of notably larger diameter than found on casting rods. Here again, though, a minimum of six very hard alloy guides denote some of the best rod construction, and the longest rods naturally will have the most guides.

Rod action, or flexibility, is an entirely different subject that must be seriously considered with the use of a rod. For example the reason for short, stout, bait casting rods is to cast efficiently and retrieve the heaviest acceptable lures. Spinning rods are designed to use intermediate to lightweight lures. This being the case, it is not prudent to expect a stiff, bass action casting rod to perform with light lures in the same fashion as a seven foot light action spinning rod, or vice versa. In this respect there are light, medium, medium heavy, and heavy action rods in all categories of tackle. Whether it is a bait casting, spinning, or spin casting outfit the compromise is a medium action. By the same token if the heaviest lures are to be used, a heavy action rod will be best, no matter the style of tackle or length of rod.

It has been my experience that no such thing exists as the all-purpose rod length and action for all Illinois fish species, or for that matter for anywhere in the nation. So first decide which of the available fish species, and the lures and baits needed to catch them, will be the objectives of your efforts. Then, shop for a rod or rods to fill these requirements.

Spin casting rods are so similar to bait casting construction that reels often are used interchangeably. The handle, rod, and guides are one and the same. Respective lengths of the two, plus the aforementioned actions, are for all practical purposes the only differences.

It has been emphasized that spin casting is the compromise between bait casting and spinning gear. Similarly, length and action of the spin casting rod are also a compromise. Generally, these rods are a little longer and more flexible than their counterparts, so as to take full advantage of casting intermediate weight to lightweight lures and baits.

Finally there are the ultralight rods. These can be regarded as specialized equipment used with all the lightest lures and baits and for the person oblivious to mental stress. While fishing for bluegill or crappie with ultralight tackle you'll quickly learn whether or not your emotions are prone to becoming unglued when, all of a sudden, a five-pound bass or huge striper slurps in that little lure. Ultralights are the berries for people who function on raw nerve. They do, however, provide the epitome of sporting thrills, especially with lightweight fish species. Candidly, let's don't permit the size of these little rods to overshadow their true capabilities. When need be, they can bring to heel very bulky fish. If you choose to indulge in the ultralight experience, just be more than vaguely aware that success or failure rides on the back of a correct line tension adjustment at the reel. And this also applies to all styles of reels.

Adjusting Line Tension

All modern reels have a mechanism that either tightens or loosens the spool. These are commonly called "drag" adjustment devices. What they do is regulate the degree of tension on the spool and thus the speed of the line as it leaves the spool. What they also do is to permit very large fish to be handled successfully without breaking the line. Enough tension or drag on the spool should be exerted so the line won't break, while at the same time this pressure fights the fish, wearing it down. Too little spool tension allows the fish to do and go where it wishes, and where it wishes to go is anywhere except toward the fisherman. Too much tension works just the opposite, and a fast, powerful surge of the fish snaps the line.

A preliminary approach to correct adjustment is simply to grab the line just ahead of the reel and pull. Before doing this, however, remember that monofilament can quickly subdivide human flesh into neatly sliced equal parts, so grab and pull carefully, particularly if you are a known bleeder. If you find that the line comes off the spool too easily, tighten the adjustment device a crank or two, repeating this until the line shows resistance to being pulled. If at first the line is too tight, obviously you'll want to reverse this procedure. Now the acid test. By stopping there, smugly complacent that your line is adjusted to whittle down the antics of Moby-Dick, you are going to stand slack-jawed sick when you set the hook and what's left of your line twangs back at you. The final, most important step in the adjustment is to have the rod in a position similar to actually playing a fish.

Most fish are lost near the boat or shoreline just prior to being landed. The reason is that in such close quarters the greatest pressure is being placed on the line and spool drags or clutches, which may be improperly adjusted to withstand this tremendous force. Usually the line breaks or the hook pulls from the fish's mouth. Either way, the loss indicates far too much spool tension. In order to avoid this probability, hold the rod in the fish-fighting position, then take a firm grip on the line and pull hard, very hard. Do this suddenly and with force, exactly the way a fish would act near the boat. Now make the adjustment accordingly. If the line is too tight, loosen it a tad to slip just before the line breaks. This, then, will catch fish for you while also maintaining your line in its original condition.

We do forget, on occasion, to check line tension. We assume that because it was alright yesterday, those little reel gremlins did not skulk in the night to mess it all up for today. So with a confident strike we set the hook on the first fish of the day, then learn that our fishing buddy played an especially harsh trick on us by directing those gremlins to our tackle. In a case like this there is nothing to do except reach out there and cooly twist the appropriate knob. Frankly, I find nothing wrong with this. And if my plan is to be frenetically busy and attentive, with both hands playing a fish of suitable size for the wall, I don't mind crying for help in regulating the drag. Under these hectic circumstances three hands are better than two,unless my partner has clumsy gorilla paws.

In summary, we have more choices of tackle styles than ever before in the history of fishing. Beginning with the rod and reel concept there has been fly fishing, then bait casting, spinning, and spin casting, and as each has come on the scene each has had its brief moment of glory "superior" to its predecessor. There is a grain of truth in this. Therein rests the underlying root of the question of which type of tackle is best. Ask this question of one devoted to bass fishing and he or she'll say that bait casting is the only choice. The answer from an angler whose favorite fish is spunky little bluegill will be fly rod. In essence four people may give an equal number of answers, which would include all four types of tackle. Choices are so varied that the fifth may name a type of tackle yet uninvented. But he or she's working on it.

I have emphasized that in my opinion the all-purpose fishing tackle has not been invented, so I hope that fifth person gets the job done. Of the four types, however, there is one which if I had to limit my tackle to just one style, would be the first choice. It would be bait casting gear. Because most fishermen are open to variety, not satisfied with sameness, they are far-traveled in their fishing adventures. Just as there are always more fish on the other side of the lake there are a lot more exceptionally hard fighting fish across the state, state lines, and national borders. If we can accept this as being representative of the Illinois angler, it is easier to accept that the cost would be prohibitive to buy special tackle for every particular trip.

The versatility of bait casting runs the gamut of using lines small enough to fish for trout on the White River in Arkansas to catching king salmon in Lake Michigan—by loading the reel with appropriate line. For fishing for the largest Florida bass to steelheads of the Northwest with bait casting gear, all that's necessary is to choose the proper size line. The Southern Illinois bass fisherman will find this same casting tackle equal to the task of handling the large fish of Canada, and even many of the intermediate-weight salt-water species. Meanwhile, closer to home, bait casting reel and rod because of their "togetherness" with the angler's hands, offer a large measure of lure-casting accuracy over short distances where precision, or lack of it, can mean the difference between a fish or nothing at all.

This is not to say that spinning or spin casting equipment won't do all of the above, if the outfit is strong enough. The average light-action tackle in this category, however, when confronted with the aforementioned work, will leave the fisherman short. My point is that at present the fisherman who owns adequate bass casting gear doesn't have to feel uneasy when planning a trip to nearly anywhere in the nation.

On the other hand, owners of spinning and spin casting tackle should give their gear serious thought. The species to be fished for, the lure or baits used, their weights, size of line that is appropriate, the kind of water to be fished (open, weedless or weeds, snags, rocks and boulders, etc.) all play an important role in the choice of rod action (light, medium, heavy), its length, and the line capacity of the reel used. These same considerations also apply to fishing right here at home, with all types of tackle.

Depth Finders

Of all the new equipment introduced to freshwater fishing during the past 20 years, the depth finder has had the greatest impact. I date the introduction of depth finders to about two decades ago because before then they were virtually unknown in Southern Illinois. The common depth finder, however, predates its use by Illinois fishermen or freshwater anglers anywhere in the nation. It was routine equipment on large vessels navigating oceans, lakes, and inland waterways. These commercial units, though, generally were cumbersome and far too expensive for the average angler to own. A depth finder made by Lowrance appeared on the fishing scene in the early 1960s. This was a compact, relatively inexpensive unit designed especially for freshwater fishermen. To say that the Lowrance Company enjoyed an overnight success would be stretching the truth. Stretching it a mile.

To my knowledge, one of the first depth finders, a portable model Lowrance, to be used on a Southern Illinois lake was used in June 1966. Bill Harkins alerted me to its presence. He called from the Play Port Marina, which he managed, to say that something very strange was taking place on Crab Orchard Lake, and it would behoove me to hurry on out. His tone was unusually urgent, so I went to the dock, having arrived within 20 minutes. Harkins explained that early in the morning two complete strangers had arrived, rented one of his fishing boats, piled it with gear, and then went out on the lake. In itself there was nothing unusual about this. Strangers rented boats all the time, so Harkins thought nothing of it. When the fishermen returned to the dock about noon, however, Harkins was awestruck by what he saw. "I couldn't believe it," he said incredulously. "Those guys brought in seven bass. Seven! And the smallest one weighed about five pounds!"

Bill Harkins ordinarily was an unruffled man not given to exaggeration. Now he was more excited than I had ever seen him. Where were the men now, I wondered. "Back on the lake," he said. "They came in, unloaded those bass, took pictures of 'em and put 'em on ice in a cooler, then had lunch and went back out." Crab Orchard in June was not water to be easily conquered by strangers, particularly during one short morning. Harkins and I shared an overwhelming curiosity about these fishermen. "And you don't know their names?"

"I heard one of them call the other one, Buck. That's all. Just Buck. Does that mean anything to you?" Buck? Buck? It struck a bell. Buck Perry! It had to be him. Perry was the only bass fishing Buck I knew about who could approach a lake like Crab Orchard and make a dent in a fish population in so little time.

A former college professor from Hickory, N.C., Buck Perry was justifiably renowned nationwide as a substantial presence in bass fishing. It was said, and perhaps rightly so, that Perry knew more about bass than any other human being. In order to put this enviable reputation in the slot it deserves, the reader will recall that in the mid-1960s as a nation we were relatively ignorant of all things to do with black bass. The late, great magazine columnist Jason Lucas was still regarded as the authority on this fish. Compared to the reams of bassy knowledge sequestered in the mind of Buck Perry, however, Lucas, who wrote in the 1930s and forties and on into 1950, was a neophyte.

Obviously, Perry didn't just wake up one morning to discover that he had been touched by the magic wand of fishing wisdom. To the contrary, through the 1940s and 50s he learned his trade the hard way, by painstaking investigation of what makes bass tick and do what they do or refuse to do. By the time I met Perry on Crab Orchard Lake that June day, he had spent so many blistering hours under reflected sunlight that his face was well wrinkled. Even those who remember the era of Jason Lucas may not be aware that when Perry decided to throw in the teacher's towel for a full-time fishing career he also became for all practical purposes the nation's first free-lance professional fisherman. Starting more than three decades ago, the unimposing North Carolina native made his living by proving that supposedly "fished out" lakes and rivers actually were victims of unknowledgeable anglers and not terminally ill from lack of fish. Generally, Perry found the opposite to be true; in many lakes there were too many fish! Perry was kept busy by fishing-resort associations and chambers of commerce who anxiously hired him to exercise his special skills on their waters. Where these waters were located or the fish species they contained were irrelevant to Perry. The resulting glowing publicity for these lakes more than justified his fees for breathing new life into these asthmatic fishing holes.

Think about that for a minute. At a time when a 10-horsepower outboard motor was considered a big pusher, and there were no high-rise swiveling boat seats, or chest-size tackle boxes, or depth finders, or bass fishing tournaments, and a TV set in every home with a fishing show on every channel was years away, and Roland Martin (the well-known professional tournament fisherman, TV show host, and hawker of products [including sunglasses]), didn't yet have ears sufficiently developed to hold sunglasses, a grizzled Southerner was squinting against the brilliant sunlight reflecting off water he was being paid to fish. Today "Perryisms" commonly infiltrate fishing language fluently spoken across the nation. The terms "structure fishing," "break lines," "fish patterns," "fish migrations" and more we hear in casual conversation were first coined by Buck Perry.

Now he and a friend were in a rented boat on Crab Orchard Lake, and Harkins and I had an urgent desire to meet them, and we didn't intend to procrastinate. Harkins was tied up at the marina, so I wheeled around toward my boat. "One more thing," Harkins yelled at my disappearing form, "they use a depth finder. One of those small, portable jobs. I saw them put it in the boat. Does that sound like your man?" Indeed it did. I had heard that Perry had even contributed to the development of the remarkable little Lowrance machine.

Perry and his friend, Don Nichols, a United Airlines pilot, of Chicago, were not hard to find. It was a weekday and few other boats were on the lake. It was my turn to be awestruck now. Their boat was anchored directly over, and they were fishing, a spot which until that moment I thought that only Al Peithman and I knew about! Even more astounding, as I approached, Nichols caught a heavy bass! Easing my boat near enough to them to introduce myself, but not so near as to disturb their fishing water, we chatted briefly and agreed to meet at the dock when their fishing day was over. That meeting was a revelation for Harkins and me.

In thirty minutes Perry told us more about the bottom structure of Crab Orchard than we thought possible for anyone to know following a single day. As unrealistic as it may appear, Perry not only told us about, but also traced a map of, hot spots he and Nichols found that Harkins, Peithman, and I didn't know existed. Using this information the following day, Peithman and I went to one of them, and on the second cast he hooked a six-pound bass! Compliments of Buck Perry, thank you.

All of this discovery in such a brief span of time was, of course, made possible by the use of a depth finder. As Perry explained it, "That little magic box may not actually catch fish for you, but it quickly eliminates structure where fish won't be, while it indicates where they should be." Perry and Nichols left Southern Illinois after catching a couple dozen bass. All fish weighing less than five pounds were returned to the water, and 10 bass weighing five to seven pounds each were kept for photographing, then cleaned and iced down.

Why did Buck Perry and Don Nichols choose to fish Crab Orchard Lake? Ironically, they were "just passing through," they said, from fishing in Tennessee to a seminar Perry was slated to conduct in Chicago. With a couple of free days, they decided to fish a little. Incidentally, if you have the opportunity to acquire one or the entire run of Buck Perry's instructional fishing books, by all means do so. As an author as well as lecturer, he has been very prolific.

Through the 1970s, Perry was an untiring lecturer conducting fishing seminars in which the depth finder always played its significant role. Widely traveled throughout the Midwest, he was hired under contract by the Illinois Department of Tourism to stage his special brand of instruction for anglers in cities and towns from Chicago to Carbondale, in the latter on the Southern Illinois University campus. When I visited Hickory, N.C., in the winter of 1980 and dropped in to see him, Perry was absent though he was reached by phone. I wasn't a bit surprised where my call reached him. He was in Florida, naturally, fishing for bass.

The interest Perry sparked in me in depth finders in 1966 burst into roaring flames, and two weeks later I owned one, and found the machine to be one of the most fascinating fishing tools I had ever used. Since then there have been astronomical improvements in these mechanisms, plus a variety of brand names from which to choose. If you can become excited over actually seeing where fish rest beneath the surface, these artistic devices will draw pictures faster than a Polaroid. These also draw heavy slack in a bank account. Digital readout or "flasher" model depth finders are much less expensive, but they do not provide a permanent record of lake bottom structure as do the graphic models.

Buying a depth finder is like acquiring any and all items of fishing equipment. It becomes a matter of individual taste, overall usefulness, and priority within the larger scheme of things, not the least of which is becoming knowledgeable about what a depth finder is doing when it does it. Read very thoroughly the operating instructions accompanying your new depth finder. The more you immediately grasp their meaning, the more time you'll spend in places where fish are, and less time where they are not, never were, and ain't gonna be. If it is true nationwide, and I suspect it's nudging the truth, that only 10 percent of the area of any and all lakes holds all of a given fish population, then to find these scarce waters is a good reason for depth finders. Exactly what kind of bottom structure you will be looking for is discussed elsewhere in this book, so I won't flog that subject to death again here.

An expedient method of finding the best bottom structure with a depth finder, however, and to determine whether fish are there at the time is to troll lures. Trolling can be especially effective on lakes that the angler is visiting for the first time. Trolling, depth finders, and topographical maps of the lake bottom are best used in combination. First study the topo map to determine places that appear promising. Then scour these likely locations with the depth finder while a lure is being trolled behind the boat.

For a working example we'll choose the typical point of land that gradually diminishes from the shoreline to beneath the surface. We have to assume, until proven otherwise with the depth finder, that the contour of this land point continues uninterrupted for at least a few yards. This form of structure on any lake anywhere is favorable fish habitat, so it is the logical target to begin exploring with the depth finder and trolled lures. Starting in shallow water just a few feet deep and gradually tracing a course back and forth over this submerged hump to its maximum depth will quickly tell you whether or not fish are there. Then, if a fish is caught, you also know at what level they hover, so you would continue to work this particular depth. This is commonly referred to as establishing a pattern with the depth finder. Tons of white bass, in particular, are caught each summer by fishermen using the above-described method. It is also used successfully for crappie, bluegill, bass, and any species that will take trolled lures.

The bass fisherman who prefers casting locates especially attractive spots by the same route, then either anchors the boat and casts or uses a trolling motor to hold the boat in position. Now, the real worth of a depth finder is appreciated. Following the discovery of a few of these fishy places it is no longer necessary to investigate aimlessly all the possible nooks and crannies offered by most lakes. A sufficient number of these productive spots keeps us busy enough fishing them. Still another argument for the depth finder is the many man-created impoundments where rivers and streams were dammed to hold back water making large lakes. This was the case with all lakes in Southern Illinois. In these waters the original river or stream beds are some of the best natural fish habitats to be found. Although they may be found far from shorelines, fish usually are living in various hard-to-find spots along these old channels. Here again, the topo map and the depth finder team up to help locate these lucrative fishing holes. Unfortunately, some Southern Illinois lakes such as Little Grassy, Devils Kitchen, and Crab Orchard were impounded without the benefit of precise topographical maps charting their depths and contours. If there is a better reason to use a depth finder to unravel the mysteries of these and other uncharted waters, I don't know about it.

As gifted as these machines are, however, they do not catch fish, and there is no way one can be trained to nudge fish into a feeding spree. Digital depth finders will help you locate what appears to be promising fish habitat, while the graphs actually mark some individual fish on paper, but catching them is an entirely different matter. To do this you are on your own.

Not only is the successful fisherman quietly confident that he or she will hook a fish with the very next cast, but there is another common trait found in those who catch the most fish; as unlikely as it may appear, they are very impatient people given to inquisitiveness. Perhaps the late Irv Peithman, of Carbondale, summed it up best. "Fishing is more hunting than just fishing," he said. "You have to hunt the fish, go where they are, and the larger the lake or river the more places there are to hunt for."

Artificial Lures

In 1772, Captain James Cook, who discovered many islands in the South Pacific, noted in his log that natives of the Sandwich Islands

(Hawaii) used a spoon-type fishing lure made from native shell. It is reasonable to assume, then, that the widespread use of artificial lures did not suddenly begin in 1772, but were in general use for decades, perhaps centuries, throughout the world before Cook and associates unfurled their sails to the winds.

Now let's jump to North America to the year 1812 where in Vermont a legendary man was born. This was Julio T. Buel, and eighteen years later Buel would be fishing near his home when he "invented" the spoon. The legend persists that, while young Buel took time off from fishing to eat lunch in his boat, he clumsily dropped a common tablespoon over the side and, as he watched it sink, a large fish suddenly dashed up to it. Following this enlightening experience, no tablespoon within reach of Buel was safe from being converted to a fishing lure. It was simple to cut off their handles, drill holes, and attach hooks.

It is obvious, though, that to credit Buel with the invention of the spoon would be unrealistic. Here again we see nothing more than an improvement of a fishing tool that, in all likelihood, predates Buel's birth by centuries. He did, however, file for the first patent in the United States to manufacture and market the spoon lure. The J. T. Buel Company opened its doors in 1848.

The word "plug" in America, evolved from the age-old ritual of whittling and spitting, thinking and idly slashing away at a chunk of wood. The founder of the well-known James Heddon tackle company is given credit for marketing one of the first widely accepted plug-type lures. The idea struck Heddon when a piece of wood he whittled on was tossed into the river and a bass struck it. That evening, Heddon whittled a realistic plug. The year was 1896, and two years later the Heddon Company was founded as a surface lure manufacturer. It would be remiss not to emphasize that James Heddon did not actually invent the plug-type lure. It had been used for a century or more in various parts of the world including England. Before 1800, British fishermen were using artificial lures called "minnows" that had the same general body shape of latter-day plugs.

Of all artificials, it appears that flies are steeped in the greatest antiquity. Historians who unearth information of this kind say that mention of artificial flies appears in the writings of scribes who lived in 250 B.C. The first mention of artificial flies being used was found in Macedonian writings. The river where they were used was called Astracus.

Detailed instructions about how to tie certain fly patterns were included in English writings about fishing, when the word was spelled "fysshynge." The fly pattern handed down through the ages which, when I discovered it, made my day complete, was called "Cowdung." Whoever invented it, I like his style.

Leaping over a few centuries, Southern Illinois has its share of lure makers. Notable among them is Haskell "Hack" Jackson, of Marion. A coal miner by profession, Jackson acquired the patent on the "Lunker Lure," the forerunner of all lures currently known as buzzbaits. Whether or not Jackson actually invented this lure is debatable by others who claim to have been the first to fashion a similar surface lure. But there is no question but what Jackson was first to patent it and market it in Southern Illinois.

It is equally unquestionable that the Lunker Lure was for many years pure Southern Illinois. I had never seen or heard of one until I moved to Carbondale in 1965. Few fishermen outside this region had either. This carefully guarded secret inevitably was divulged by anglers of the region traveling in particular through southern Georgia to Florida. Wherever it was taken, the Lunker Lure left an indelible impression. On Lake Seminole in Georgia, for instance, we used the Lunker Lure one year, and the following year we saw a number of fishermen using this same lure, which they had put together in their basements.

It was with the Lunker Lure that Bill McCabe, of Marion, while on Lake Jackson in Florida, caught the first 14-pound largemouth bass most Southern Illinoisans had ever seen. The following year, Bill Harkins and this writer caught our first 9- and 10-pound bass with Lunker Lures when fishing the same Florida lake near Tallahassee. This piece of fish-catching hardware indisputably caused southern state anglers to make identical copies.

The reason they were forced to make their own stemmed from the inability of Jackson to keep up with demand. Each lure was handmade, and its popularity with anglers throughout Southern Illinois left no room for its maker to accumulate a stockpile from one season to the next. There is a persisting story, in fact, about how men formed lines outside the Jackson kitchen door to buy Lunker Lures even before the paint had dried. For the times, the mid to late 1960s, the price of a Lunker Lure at $2.50 was outrageously steep. The average lure was priced below $1.00. But this was not your basic average lure, so cost was relative. It is interesting to note that today from one large mail-order catalog buzzbaits similar in all respects to the Lunker Lure can be purchased for only $2.00.

As we are fully aware, there is a proliferation of claims and counter-claims for having made the "original" of about every known product. In this respect the Lunker Lure is a product of Southern Illinois, specifically from Marion, and it was the original from which all similar buzzbaits were copied. The same cannot be said of spinner baits. To my knowledge no one knows who or where the first lures of this type were used. Spinner baits are probably offspring of the spoon-type lures first made of shell. In all likelihood metal was substituted where seashells were not readily available. If shell was good, polished metal was better, more durable, and longer lasting.

Spinner baits in general are the most made and the most copied by more people than any other lure type. Today there is a bewildering number of spinner bait makers, and tomorrow there will be more. This is why it is impossible to single out one or two Southern Illinois makers of this type lure. By the time this work is published those mentioned may no longer be in business while others may spring up to take their place.

Despite the immensity of competition, one of the first spinner bait lures of its kind introduced to the American angler following World War II not only endures but steadily grows in popularity on the international market. This one is the Mepps Spinner made in Antigo, Wisconsin. The man who brought it from France to this country, Todd Sheldon, still heads the Mepps Company, a family-owned business. Thus it can be safely said that the varieties of Mepps Spinners were the forerunners of most similar lures which followed.

This does not mean, however, that everyone duplicated Mepps lures. To the contrary, spinner bait styles were and are as variable as the regions they are used in, and a few styles have become nearly localized concepts. Of the international marketing manufacturers, perhaps the second largest is Warden's, of Granger, Washington, which makes Rooster Tails. Formerly known as the Yakima Bait Company because of its proximity to the nearby Yakima River, Warden's enjoys a healthy share of the domestic spinner bait market, particularly in western states.

The most recent addition to the types of fishing lures is the plastic worm introduced by Nick Creme, founder of the Creme Lure Company, of Tyler, Texas. Creme got the idea to market a plastic version of a live nightcrawler three-hook rig used during the late 1940s by Minnesota and Ontario, Canada, walleye fishermen. The first Creme plastic worms closely resembled those made by hand in the North Country. The worm was spread out over three hooks and at the forward end Creme added a small propeller to generate more action to the lure. Between the propeller and worm head were beads which allowed free movement for the propeller's rotation.

Obviously, this lure was designed to be retrieved steadily and fast enough to activate the propeller. The inherent problem was in the three exposed hooks. This design had the hooks stuck all the way through the plastic worm; thus they attracted snags as well as fish. The "Texas rig" eliminated two of the original hooks while also leaving the barb of the single hook inside the body of the plastic worm, making the lure significantly snag-free compared to the Creme design. This new idea left off the propeller as well as taking advantage of improved, softer plastic used for making plastic worms. Finally, the Texas rig was weighted with a cone-shaped sinker at the head.

The Flip Tail plastic worm made in Georgia by the Stembridge Company was one of the first with improved, comparatively soft plastic conducive to leaving the barb of the hook embedded in the worm body. Prior to that time plastic worms were far too tough to rely on the hook's penetrating both the worm and the jaw of a bass. Flip Tails were the first plastic worms widely used in Southern Illinois, and the Texas rig with slip sinker and single hook was the one most used. The introduction came about 1967, but acceptance of this drastic departure from the norm was exceptionally slow in coming.

At that time three lures held sway as the most popular—the Lunker Lure for spring surface fishing, the spinner bait for both spring and early summer, and the Bomber for fishing summer bass in deep water. All three were action lures, requiring physical activity from the fisherman who viewed anything less demanding with unexpressed contempt. Some openly expressed their distaste for these newfangled do-nothing plastic worms. One of them was a man who later would become one of the best plastic worm fishermen in Southern Illinois. "Those things are no better than using live nightcrawlers," John Swetz sniffed when I suggested that he give plastic worms a try. "I'll stick to spinner baits. They catch fish." Swetz scoffed flatly at the plastic worm nonsense.

It would be a full year before Swetz reluctantly decided that just maybe his initial assessment of plastic worms had been hasty, probably based on faithfulness to spinner baits which had stood him in good stead for so many years. When Swetz and his Royalton-based teammates won the prestigeous Southern Illinois Bass Fishing Team Championship the first time it was their manipulation of plastic worms which pulled it off. It was also plastic worms which made this Royalton team the only one in the history of this annual event to win it three consecutive years.

My devotion to plastic worms for summer bass was the reason that Al Peithman and I stopped fishing so often together. Peithman was equally faithful to Bombers, and with this lure he could literally overwhelm my efforts with plastic worms. For every cast I make he would fire a dozen, covering the area like hair on a horse, then he would be eager to up anchor and move on. These lures used from the same boat are totally incompatible.

The first so-called crank bait was whittled out of balsa wood by a Kentuckian who ended up with a lure much like a pregnant guppie. This was an instant winner. Bass fishermen clamored for the lure, so the maker hired a battery of skilled whittlers and spitters to comply with orders flooding in.

Being fickle creatures by nature, fishermen ignored the fact that a number of lures available for years were most effective when cranked furiously on retrieve, yet the name "crank bait" somehow eluded them. But now, suddenly, this fat little lure with the low-slung belly was dubbed with the name which all that followed would be called. A variety of crank baits certainly did follow, and without delay. Within a couple years there were nearly as many brands of crank baits as there were spinner baits, with names ranging from Balsa-B to the Wee-R. It was natural to call all lures of this type the "alphabet series."

In reality they were and are plugs with solid bodies differing only in shape and paint jobs from the one first cut with a pocket knife by James Heddon. It is ironic, too, that it took more than seventy years for another man with another pocket knife to whittle out a Balsa-B which stirred so much emotion among the bass fishing fraternity. Tournament anglers were driven to carrying their precious Balsa-B lures in egg cartons to prevent chipping their delicately painted designs. As I said at the outset, there is nothing really new in fishing tackle, particularly in the area of lures. I'll wager that a piece of glimmering conch shell is as effective as anything for fooling fish. I know for a fact that tabs from beer cans are. More importantly, I wonder what happened to that old fly called Cowdung?

Plastic Worms and Rods Used

Plastic worms are being treated separately because they are a category unto themselves. There is no other lure quite like them, and they are unquestionably the most difficult of all artificials for the beginner to become thoroughly acquainted with. Ironically, plastic worms were looked upon with disdain in their infancy; but since then this type lure has enjoyed a popularity increase among the army of the nation's bass fishermen while less enduring lures have dropped to the also-ran category.

The average bass lure has a life-span of about three years to reach its peak. This means the majority of lures hit the market like gang busters and rise to an often phenomenal sales rate for about two years, after which their attractiveness to fickle bass anglers declines just as rapidly, or at best sales level off. Then most popular lures maintain a measure of steadiness, their sales neither rising much or falling alarmingly, until something new and perhaps revolutionary is introduced. When these introductions catch on they blaze like wildfire.

This does not imply that lures used 20 or 30 years ago to catch bass are less effective today. Some of the best we knew in the 1960s are still around and being flung. Two which pop to mind are the original Lazy Ike, introduced about 1947, and the staid old Jitterbug made by the Fred Arbogast Company. The reason these two remain uppermost in memory is that my first largemouth bass caught with a subsurface artificial was with a Lazy Ike in the same year it was first marketed. The first bass I ever caught with a surface lure smacked a Jitterbug.

Dozens of lures, many of them unchanged, made by a number of tackle companies in the 1940s are alive and healthy and still catching their share of fish. But overall comparison between increased use of plastic worms for 1960 through today with other types of lures shows worms winning going away.

Although they were first greeted with something less than lukewarm enthusiasm, plastic worms have to receive credit for the training of millions of bass fishermen. When these lures are fished correctly they are quite deadly nearly all months of the year on any water in the country that contains bass.

Of first importance is that most fishermen who use these weighted lures accept the fact that to be successful they must be fished on or near the bottom. This thinking alone is contradictory to the old belief that largemouth bass could be taken with surface lures sometimes and shallow-running subsurface lures the rest of the time—and only when they were interested. Before plastic worms were developed, bass anglers were content with the misinformed notion that if fish were not interested in a floating or running type lure they must be in semihibernation. So ninety-nine out of a hundred fishermen failed to attempt to fish lures deep enough to locate bass.

The worm turned, literally. "No matter how deep the water, you have to fish plastic worms on the bottom," was one of the first phrases I recall hearing about plastic worms. Perhaps this characteristic is one of the reasons plastic worms were slow in gaining acceptance. Oriented to casting and cranking to stay busy, the average fisherman simply did not want to waste what he or she felt was valuable time in fishing a lure so slowly. To those unacquainted with plastic worms, catching bass that way was unnecessary, nor were bass as deep as some people said they were, anyway. Time and persistence proved that fish were indeed "that deep" most of the time, in all but a brief period in spring during the spawning season. By dedicated probing of these depths with lead-weighted plastic worms even in the hottest months, fishermen with a penchant for experimentation began to disprove many of the age-old bass fishing beliefs. They caught fish. How they caught fish!

Original widespread thoughts about how fish take plastic worms had them sneaking up behind the lure to first nip it on the tail, then to slowly gobble in the rest of the worm, something like sucking in a string of spaghetti. In Texas some innovative angler refused to believe that bass took worms this way. He replaced the three-hook rig with a single hook near the head of the worm. To his delight, all the bass he caught had sucked in the head with the hook just as he had noticed all bass doing with the three-hook setup.

When a fish takes a lure or live food he opens his gill plates simultaneously with his mouth. At this point the mechanical food intake gears are meshed and a suction is created, pulling water into the mouth and out the flared gill plates. Anything within range of open-mouthed suction is quickly drawn into the cavity. Once the food, or lure, is inside this trap the gates are slammed shut. Many fish go through the same mouth opened—gills flared motion to clear away silt and parasites from gills. This is also one reason fish jump and slash above the surface. They are not "romping and playing with great fun" as antifishing folks would have children believe.

With the plastic worm inside the gaping maw of the fish, the only question left for the angler is when to set the hook. It should be immediately. But first, let's go through our own fishing motions with the plastic worm before we arrive at that critical hook-setting moment.

When the plastic worm hits the surface, keep your eyes glued to the line where it enters the water. Many bass pick up a worm lure as it falls, and a telltale twitching of the line indicates this has happened. If it does, set the hook fast and hard. If nothing unusual occurs, the worm is permitted to sink to the bottom. This is indicated by the line's becoming limp. Reel in slack line as the rod tip is raised, and be alert. Bass also often take a plastic worm just as it strikes bottom. If there is unnatural pressure holding the lure, again, set the hook. This could be a fish.

In the beginning usage of plastic worms, assume absolutely nothing is or is not a bass until it proves out one way or the other. The safest way is to rare up and set the hook. You might feel a little sheepish when there is nothing down there, but this won't disturb you nearly as much as missing an opportunity to hook a large fish.

Rod position is extremely important to success. Keep the rod high. At the lowest point it should not drop below 45 degrees or thereabouts. From this position work it up to about 90 degrees, and while the rod swings up the lure is being moved across the bottom. The reason the rod tip should not be too low is because of essential time required for the angler to prepare once the hit is felt. For example, let's say the rod is pointed downward and the tip is aimed directly at the fish. When the pickup of the plastic worm comes it will be so sudden that the bass feels the resistance of the tight line. Real worms and small snakes don't resist this way, and before the startled angler can react the bass has forcefully ejected the lure.

Repeat the up and down motion of the rod, and each time reel slack line to the spool, keeping a relatively tight line. This is the only way you'll be able to feel the slightest peck through the line and rod when a bass sucks in the plastic worm. This light touch will feel like no more than that of a bluegill or other small fish. Actually, what the bass has done is eased up to the lure, decided it is palatable, and opened his mouth and gills to suck it in. That discernable peck one feels is the bass closing his mouth, with the hook end of the lure inside. When this occurs, lower the rod immediately while cranking up all available slack line. With no slack left in which to lose the hook-setting power, pull straight up, hard and fast, with the rod. You will need all the power you can muster. The hook you are using is gussied up with a colorful plastic worm. The point of the hook is lodged inside this plastic to make the lure weedless, snag-free. There is also some inherent stretch in monofilament line. All of this must be overcome with the violence of the thrust, which causes the barb to penetrate sufficiently the bony jaw of bass.

Unfortunately, there are no shortcuts to learning how bass and other fish treat plastic worms. With any other type lure, generally, we know when fish strike; they send a clear message through the line and rod. We receive this unquestionable signal because action type lures, which are in motion, suddenly stop and perhaps vibrate with life at the end of the line. Nothing of the sort happens with plastic worm fishing, unless the hit comes as a complete surprise to the angler, at which time it might be too late. Trophy-size bass that everyone wants to brag about catching are often cautious. They won't wait too long for a startled angler to recover his senses and set the hook. These fish disgorge plastic worms with the speed of a pellet from a high-pressure air rifle. These unexpected strikes, or pickups, can be expected by the astute plastic worm caster when the lure is in two different situations: first, just after it touches bottom and before a tight line indicates the bass has accepted it; and secondly, the worm is somewhere between the bottom and the boat as it is being brought up for the next trip through the air.

In the first situation all the angler might feel is a dullness, a blah type sensation neither alive nor dead, though something obviously holds the lure. This indescribable something might suddenly turn into an awakened giant of a fish. It took in the lure and stayed right there, unmoving, with the intention of swallowing it. There was no reason for the fish to go anywhere, carrying off the plastic worm. Big fish do not needlessly waste energy.

The first hint you might have that a fish has the lure is when you raise the rod and feel pressure on the line. The next thing you might see is the line slicing a groove in the surface as the fish heads toward deep water. Finally, you set the hook and discover that, astonishingly enough, the fish has already carried your lure and line beneath the boat. This is an especially difficult position from which to get a hook firmly set in a bass. It would have been far better to have jabbed the suspect fish at the very beginning, even if the hunch failed to prove out.

Another common sneak attack on a worm comes as the bass just happens to see it a few feet before the lure is lifted from the water at the end of a cast. He hits it like it's the only thing between him and starvation. Without the slightest warning, the angler feels a sudden jolt, the rod dips alarmingly, and if the angler is really lucky and quick he or she might catch this fish.

Of all positions assumed by plastic worms when they encourage fish to snatch them, the most common is at the bottom when they are being moved. Generally, the worm makes contact with bottom structure, then, as it is first lifted by the rod and line and wiggles enticingly away, the bass grabs it. If this doesn't take place in the first movement or two it will soon thereafter, if a fish has set up residence there.

Whether or not this ever has appeared in print before now, I can't be certain, though I haven't seen it mentioned that nine times out of ten worm fishermen can tell by the way they hit when a bass is desirably large or throw-back small. Small fish really work at assaulting a plastic worm. Hefty bass take it in almost haughty stride. Bass of one pound or so bite plastic worms in a series of quick spurts. The sensation coming to the hands through the rod is nearly a rat-tat-tat, like a greyhound nipping at the heels of a rabbit.

Conversely, confident bass of size and authority move on the plastic worm with one fell swoop. The message received by the angler is a single chomp. Just one, no more. It is just a clunk, like the closing of a bank vault. In Costa Rica, I have caught 60-pound tarpon that pecked lures no more vigorously than do bass taking plastic worms. In fact, the sensation I received to my hands when tarpon of 40 pounds upward sucked in a lure slowly dragged over the bottom reminded me of a large bass chomping down on plastic worms.

The point is that the larger the fish about to eat an easily caught food the less excited it becomes. It is easy for them to do this while smaller fish, always in competition with others, must work their little tails off grasping at every opportunity. The most opportune time to stick a bass that has inhaled a plastic worm is well defined. You do it at once without delay. When you feel the peck, get ready, then whop it to him.

There was a time, however, and not too many years ago, when the average plastic worm fisherman wasn't so all-fired certain that a sudden move was the best move. Many anglers even let fish run off line, perhaps yards of line, before their rods went skyward. Although the best move is an immediate hook set, some bass, given time, will start to eat these lures. Give them enough time and they will finish the job.

Plastic worms made today are so lifelike, so palatable to fish, they will eat them, and they will eat them right off the hooks snagged and broken off on stumps and other brushy places. I can't recall how many bass I've caught that, when cleaned, had old pastic worms in their stomachs. To be sure, these were color-faded, undigested plastics which in time would be dislodged or dissolved by the fish's powerful digestive juices. But when a bass will eat the trimmings right off the tree it does give us some notion of just how attractive these lures are to them. Year-round the plastic worm is unquestionably the fish-catchingest device fishermen have ever seen.

It would be remiss in our discussion of plastic worms not to mention rods used with such lures. Not all rods are suitable; some rod actions defeat the entire effort. Everything evolves around signals from fish transmitted to the hands of the fisherman. Oftentimes, success in using plastic worms depends as much or more on a sense of feel as it does on visual contact. You have to recognize that discernible touch when fish close their mouths on such worms. One would think that long, flexible, sensitive rods would transmit these signals no matter how light the fish's touch, and to a certain degree they do. Actually, though, the identification is much better through a stout rod with a medium to heavy action.

Knowing that a fish has glommed down on the lure is only the beginning of a two-part sequence before it is securely hooked. The second, critical, stroke is combining enough force with rod action to overcome the line's natural stretch and drive the hook through the plastic worm into the fish's tough mouth. More often than not this striking force is neutralized within a long, skinny, flexible shaft.

The first "worm action rods" were beefed-up casting models. Much of their stiffness was incorporated in their butt sections and the tapers to tips were less pronounced than on medium to light action rods. Bulk meant weight, of course, so many fiberglass worm rods were pretty hefty sticks. Perhaps we didn't realize how heavy these were until the introduction of graphite. This material was amazingly light and dimensionally smaller than fiberglass in all respects. More important, the sensitivity of graphite was significantly more pronounced in announcing a hit on plastic worms. The exceptionally fast tip response of graphite was, and still is, a bonus when the hook is set.

No matter the material it is made of, however, a rod designed for plastic worm fishing generally is the wise choice over all others. Also, the two- or three-rod plastic worm fisherman should give serious thought to matching them—same length, same action, and made by one manufacturer. Otherwise, rods can be as different as ZIP codes. Switch from one to the other and strangeness sets in like an unemployed relative. Plastic worm fishermen need fewer, not more, handicaps keeping them in the dark. Speaking of darkness, one black night on a lake will do more for your education than a full season of daylight casting these plastics. When you must totally rely on feel you'll quickly cull the touch of inanimate objects compared with the zesty tap of a bass.

When you get this message, set the hook as though you intend to break the rod. Quality will stand the gaff, so it is rare when a rod actually breaks under this kind of pressure. It does happen, though. I've lost count of the rods I've broken while actually fishing. They are so many that I'm looking forward to discovering new and exciting ways to shatter more of them, and opportunities will no doubt present themselves while using plastic worms. That rods take a lot of abuse is good enough reason to get those made especially for this work. It's an uncommon happening, though, when the weight of a fish is responsible for rod breakage. Giving manufacturers their due, there is superb quality in today's quality fishing rods, so generally it's angler neglect which causes the eventual fracture of glass or graphite when a hook is set on fish.

When we consider the many ingenious ways to damage rods with numerous little nicks and cracks to which we pay no heed, it's no wonder that rods subdivide in our hands at inopportune times. The most insignificant appearing nick can be like a thumb-size hole in a dam; it's going to swell until it bursts. Letting a rod hammer against one sharp edge can do more damage to it than all the fish in Southern Illinois.

With a single exception, the length of rod is unimportant. The hook-setting arc of a six-foot rod is less than that of any rod of shorter length. Compare this by imagining the rod is long enough to reach to just above the fish no matter how deep it might be. It would take a short jerk, then, to set the hook. Now, picture the more exaggerated image of trying to slam home a barb with one of those midget pocket outfits advertised on TV. You would have to charter an airplane to match the rise of a six-foot casting rod. Many graphite rods are made in especially funny lengths, anywhere from five feet two inches over-all to six feet. I can't explain these odd measurements and I've never had the courage to ask, fearing that I'll find manufacturers employing two-headed orangutans to make these weird selections. Meanwhile, keep flinging those plastics and hope they don't settle too often on the far side of stumps.

Live Worms

Of all things real or artificial used for fishing nothing quite compares with the lowly worm for producing satisfactory results. It is the rare fish that will not eat a worm. Still more rare is the angler who did not catch his or her first fish with a worm-baited hook. It's interesting that the typical progression of fishing techniques, tackle, and baits generally begins with using live worms, then on to artificial lures. We come to believe that lures are the more sporting way, the greater challenge fulfilled, whenever fish are fooled by them. Ironically, this so-called progress also includes a deep-rooted attitude of some contempt, though not openly expressed, of people who have not advanced their ways and who still use live worms. It's a form of fishing snobbery hidden in every bubble-packed artificial lure. Notice the reaction when on any lake in the land someone brings in a batch of fish big enough to feed a village of Eskimos all winter. Every angler present wants to know where on the lake they were caught and what these fish were caught with. If an artificial was used, everyone is delighted, and that manufacturer's stock goes up 10 percent. Conversely, it is a tragic development akin to the *Titanic*'s going down if people learn that live nightcrawlers were the bait.

In truth, the worm suffers an unwarranted reputation. Not only will it do things for fishermen that pieces of metal, plastic, or wood won't and can't do, but the worm really is a giant of a little creature. It is both male and female processing common soils through its body to be ejected as especially rich fertilizers. A great deal of the earth's top-soil is manufactured by worms. It is common knowledge that for their size ants have the strength of raging bulls. Compared to the average worm, the ant is a 98-pound weakling who has sand kicked in his face at the beach. When a nightcrawler flexes its muscles, fire ants cringe, the ground shudders, and boulders are moved aside.

As George Sroda, the Wisconsin scientist who perhaps knows as much or more about nightcrawlers than any person, says about his life's work: "Worms, not dogs, are man's best friend. They don't bark and wake the neighbors, they don't have to be housebroken or dutifully taken for walks. They don't shed hair on the carpet, track in mud, or slobber all over you."

As Sroda also pointed out one day when I visited him in his Wisconsin laboratory: "Nightcrawlers are totally undemanding. All you have to do to keep them satisfied is keep them cool and moist in temperatures between 45 and 55 degrees. Let them get too warm, though, and they shrivel. Yech! It's a mess."

"Protein!" Sroda suddenly blurted. "Nightcrawlers are loaded with it. Did you know that in California a woman is compiling data for a book about cooking with worms?"

I didn't know.

"Yes," Sroda said. "I've had a number of conversations with her. You can use worms in all sorts of cooking, and they are excellent. We use them all the time." As an afterthought, Sroda suddenly picked up a plate of cookies which had been on his desk. "Here," he said. "Have one. They are nice sugar cookies baked by my wife."

"Uh, no thank you, George. I'm not much on sugar cookies."

"Oh, please try them. You'll love 'em," Sroda insisted, taking one for himself. "My wife's a fine cook, and this is her newest recipe."

"Uh, George, do they have, ah, you know? Are they made with, uh, maybe the recipe came from, well, California?"

"As a matter of fact they are," he munched the cookie. "How did you know?"

"Just a lucky guess. Uh, no thanks, George. I just ate a 10-pound steak and I'm a little stuffed right now."

"Oh, come now. Don't be squeamish. These are delightful. Simply delightful," he took another cookie. "My wife will be offended if you don't try them."

I didn't particularly care whether or not I offended someone I had never met and probably never would. For all I knew those cookies were mailed to Sroda directly from the West Coast. I visualized the package squirming at 30,000 feet over Omaha.

But Sroda continued to toss down cookies like popcorn, and I was running out of excuses. Finally, I relented and took one, nibbling tentatively at its edge, just a polite nip. After all, Sroda had not admitted that the cookies contained, well, those things. He was right. His wife showed a masterful skill as a baker. The cookie was superb. I ate the whole thing. To this day I don't know all the ingredients in those cookies. And I don't want to know. Naturally, there is a lingering suspicion, particularly when I get that nearly uncontrollable urge to bore holes in the lawn.

Protein for human consumption aside, worms will catch fish for you. From bluegill to bass, rainbow trout to walleye and the catfishes, most species in Southern Illinois gobble up worm-baited hooks. The knowledge of degree of gobble of different species of fish is what separates experienced worm anglers from the also-rans who throw only artificial lures. Those schooled in worming are fine-tuned to the ways various species of fish take this bait. For example, seldom will any fish greedily snatch a worm and dash away. First, fish cautiously investigate either by smell, sight, or both before taking a sample. Fish invented the word "nibble," and small channel catfish must have come by the name "fiddler" because of their exasperating habit of fiddling around with live nightcrawlers.

The point is that it takes great skill and patience for the angler to know exactly when to strike. Hit prematurely and the fish isn't hooked. Wait too long and the fish strips away the bait, leaving you amazed at how they can do this and avoid that hook. The most notorious bait stealers are the catfish. Any trotline or jug fisherman can give testimony about the overbalance of baits lost in relation to fish caught. One would also think that a fish with a mouth as ferocious as the walleye would charge up to a worm, snap it into forty-some-odd pieces, and eat the residue. To the contrary, of all species the walleye is one of the slowest, most cautious live worm eaters. Nonetheless it can hardly resist eating them.

As George Sroda emphasized, it is essential to keep live worms cool and moist, but not wet, if they are to perform at peak capacity. Packed in damp soil mixed with shredded papers in a spacious container placed on ice or in the refrigerator will maintain them in good shape for weeks. Or, the alternative is to buy one of the commercial worm beddings, then store the worms the same way as Sroda suggested. Unfortunately, the Illinois variety of nightcrawler does not reproduce naturally in the captivity of a refrigerator or other confined places. From time to time the supply will have to be replenished. It is also a dismaying fact that most of the soil covering Southern Illinois does not contain nightcrawlers, though there are isolated pockets of them scattered here and there. These are token populations, however, compared to those in the black-soil belt of Illinois, northern states, and Canada.

Even at today's prices buying fishing worms is a bargain in relation to the cost of a tackle box brimming over with artificial lures. The average live worm user could fish all season for the cost alone of some tackle boxes. Then, too, bigger worms are not always better. Appropriate nightcrawler size depends on the relative size of fish to be caught. Generally, all that's necessary is to have enough bait to cover the hook, dress it up in disguise. It is also a general rule that large fish show more interest in large baits than in small ones.

The largest nightcrawler I've ever seen, perhaps the world's largest which never will become fish food, is Herman the Worm. Herman is a national TV celebrity who travels with George Sroda to make numerous personal appearances each year. This pampered 16 incher has been introduced by every talk show host from Johnny Carson to Merv Griffin, and Sroda has lost track of the countless newspaper articles written about the two of them. One of these stories appeared in the *Southern Illinoisan* soon after that unsettling cookie episode in Sroda's office. Despite his obvious affection for his devoted companion, Herman, Sroda is not a fanatic antifisherman or a member of any Save the Worm movement. Far from it, he says. "I've given my life to worms and to informing fishermen about them, how to care for them, and how to use them to best advantage. Why, the proudest moment in my life is when I can tell people, I've got worms."

5.

Tournaments and Clubs,
Trophies and Taxidermy

Tournaments and Clubs

The first organized bass fishing tournament was staged on Crab Orchard Lake in the late 1960s. It was named the Southern Illinois Bass Fishing Team Championship. This is the same annual contest which today is known as the Bill Harkins Memorial Tournament. The late Bill Harkins, of Carterville, was especially instrumental in launching this four-man team contest. Although at the outset most of the participants were from Southern Illinois, in later years this event would involve bass fishermen from the length and breadth of Illinois. It would also become a closely copied prototype upon which other nearby state team championships would be based.

This contest was the result of a similar event this writer attended on Greers Ferry Lake, Arkansas, on a cold, blustery December day. I was there to meet and fish with Glenn Andrews, a tournament promoter and former professional guide whose fishing fame was widespread. A tall, lean Arkansan from Rogers, Glenn Andrews had the reputation among professional guides of being nearly unbeatable in bass fishing competition. I knew that one day on Bull Shoals Lake in Arkansas, Andrews had generously given his fishing competition an unprecedented four-hour head start to go on the lake and catch bass. Then he jumped in his boat and went fishing. Incredibly enough Andrews won that contest! Obviously, I was anxious to meet Glenn Andrews, and I was impressed by what I saw, particularly his efficient management of the event, which featured two-man teams. Despite the harsh weather, bass weighing up to four pounds were caught. The enthusiasm of contestants to spend bone-chilling, arduous hours flinging lures was sufficient reason for me to ponder whether this same tournament format would be accepted in Southern Illinois.

A few days later Bill Harkins and I discussed it at the Play Port Marina, which he managed, on Crab Orchard Lake. He was enthused about putting together a team tournament, so we visited Loren Taylor, the owner-manager of the Gateway Marina, also on Crab Orchard. After hearing our ambitious plan, Taylor didn't hesitate in approving it. "Let's do it," he said. So, then and there, Harkins, Taylor, and I became a committee of three to work out the details for launching this tournament.

Although the Greers Ferry contest headed by Andrews was not a statewide event, ours would be. In place of two-man teams we would have four men per team, spreading the modest entry fee cost so more people would be interested in participating. Fortunately, we were permitted to hammer out the necessary publicity essential to announcing this contest in my daily newspaper columns for the *Southern Illinoisan*.

In our view that first tournament was a tremendous success. As I recall there were about 45 teams entered. In retrospect the equipment used in that contest was far more interesting than the number of fish weighed in, which I don't remember, anyway. Recalling that this was a period before modern bass boats with two-story motors hung on their sterns, at that time a large fishing outboard was a 25 horsepower. The average fishing vessel was a 12-foot jonboat. This was easily hoisted on and off a car top or slid into the back of a pickup truck, and boats of this kind were the dominate craft used in this first tournament. Not all of the fishing teams even owned boats! Harkins and Taylor rented every boat available from both marinas, and Harkins borrowed another dozen or more from the Little Grassy Lake boat dock. All these were used in the tournament.

It was an era when bass fishing tournaments were virtually unknown. An organization called BASS (Bass Anglers Sportsmen's Society), which would become a national giant, was then in its infancy. It would be a few years before Ray Scott, the driving force behind BASS, would promote some of the largest cash tournaments staged in the nation.

Meanwhile, Southern Illinois has its annual team championship on

Crab Orchard Lake. The second year the number of participants doubled, then in later years the numbers grew until there were so many participants that the 7,000-acre Crab Orchard Lake could not comfortably accommodate the mass of boats. By 1971, Loren Taylor had sold the Gateway Marina, leaving Harkins and myself to agonize over this glut of fishermen.

It was customary for Arch Mehrhoff, the Project Manager of the Crab Orchard National Wildlife Refuge, to send contestant boats skittering at the shot of a gun. When Mehrhoff saw the throng of 1971 boats revved up for the start, he shook his head. "You guys have created a monster," he said grinning. "Keep this up and you'll have to move this tournament to the Pacific Ocean." Mehroff didn't exaggerate. That year there were so many boats clogging the water that many anglers went to the center of the lake and anchored, staying there all day. To find a spot unoccupied by another boat, particularly near shoreline, was an exercise in futility. The problem solved itself. Bass fishermen do not like to be hemmed in. Therefore, the quickest way to reduce a given population of bass anglers is to squeeze them vice-like into confined areas they know have been whipped to a froth by the lures of others. The following year the number of teams enrolled had culled themselves down to less than wall-to-wall boats on Crab Orchard Lake.

It is clear that all tournaments in Southern Illinois are an outgrowth of the Crab Orchard Lake event. Notable among them is the annual two-man team contest held on Devils Kitchen Lake, an event flowering in the early 1970s. To my knowledge the DK contest is the only one in Southern Illinois that holds the dubious distinction of being canceled because of deep snow and solid ice. The storm that caused this originated in eastern Colorado, where I happened to be at the time.

Three of my sons—Steve, Mike, and Matthew—and I were with Barry Barker, who was producer/director of our TV series, en route from filming shows on Lake Obregón in Mexico. As we crossed the Colorado-Kansas border, a blizzard from the northwest howled at our tracks, and we barely managed to stay ahead of it. When we reached Carbondale, the storm caught up at the same time the annual Devils Kitchen bass tournament was in progress. Not only is it uncharacteristic for Southern Illinois to measure a great snowfall in April, it is unseemly for snow to shut down a fishing tournament. This one did. The day was bitter cold, windy, and launching ramps on DK were iced over. When all boats were skidded from the water to trailers, tournament officials prudently terminated the event a day short of its usual two-day duration.

There was substantial impact on tourism in Southern Illinois as a result of these two tournaments. In the annual Crab Orchard event dozens of towns and cities were represented; Chicago, Kankakee, Champaign-Urbana, Decatur, Mattoon, Danville, and Effingham are just a few of the upstate cities that sent fishing teams to compete on Crab Orchard. The Devils Kitchen affair was not restricted to Illinois residents, so out-of-state tourism was enhanced by this annual contest. For the first time in its quiet, rather secretive history the many lakes with their bountiful fishing potential in this region were becoming well known to fishermen in and out of Illinois.

Generally, fishing clubs did and still do promote and operate these tournaments. The Crab Orchard Lake Bass Club is responsible for management of the four-man team championship on Crab Orchard. In later years this club also would stage annual Boy Scout benefit contests, raising a substantial amount of money for the scouting group. The Little Egypt Bass Club sponsored the DK event.

A dark shadow hanging over the early tournaments was the number of bass killed for want of the equipment and knowhow to keep them alive. By today's standards, boats of the 1960s were archaic. Since there were no live wells, lacing fish on stringers was the norm, and also there was the widespread practice of putting a caught bass on ice to prevent precious ounces from melting away. Either way the fish died. The early tournaments were held before what would become the well-known "bass boat" with its sophisticated live well system to keep fish alive was developed. The Ranger bass boat, conceived by Forrest Wood, of Flippin, Arkansas, was just beginning to be marketed. This would go on to become one of the most popular fishing boats during the 1970s. Meanwhile, the short- and long-term mortality factors are entirely different. What you see at the weigh-in site is not necessarily what you get. When fish are caught and roughly handled, they suffer a variety of injuries including traumatic shock. Although a bass may appear to be uninjured, it could die within days or hours after being returned to the water. This was undeniably determined by fisheries biologists who studied the Crab Orchard contest. Though on-site mortality (short-term) appeared to be very low, fish that were transported in large holding tanks to the little Grassy Hatchery for observation revealed a staggering death rate—as great as 50 percent—within a period of two weeks!

Regulations and methods of handling tournament-caught bass changed for the better in the 1970s. If it was the goal of Forrest Wood to have a Ranger boat on a trailer parked in every fisherman's driveway, he came very close to that accomplishment. By 1975 many tournament regulations clearly stipulated that all contestants use boats with proper live wells. The next step was to use large plastic bags. Bass were carried in these bags, which were partially filled with lake water, from boats to the weigh-in site, thus minimizing injury to fish.

Today, of course, tournaments and bass boats are as common as crabgrass. Nearly every lake large enough to accommodate this popular exercise has at least one annual tournament. The cash incentives for competing in these contests have been greatly improved, too. During the infancy of professional tournaments it was impossible for anyone to make a living through fishing. Although it has been light-years in coming, sizable cash purses coupled with the number and frequency of tournaments across the nation make it possible for a few people to earn decent annual incomes. Even these few, however, do not rely entirely on tournament winnings to buy groceries. For the most part, winners of Southern Illinois contests usually are delighted enough with the extra cash and the warm feeling of being at the time the very best. Even today there is not enough money offered in all combined tournaments to match just a couple typical purses split amongst golfers on the PGA tour.

Some professional bass fishermen are or were employed full time on public-relations staffs of fishing tackle manufacturers, boat and trailer builders, and manufacturers of other products related to fishing. Others were fishing guides first and tournament anglers as a by-product of the profession. Still others were and are established in successful businesses that lend themselves to time and funds to compete in tournaments. We must remember that despite their current fame and apparent fortunes the best known of the pros started as rank novices.

For example, I was told by a man who was a friend of both men that when Bill Dance decided to embark on a professional tournament-fishing career he called on Glenn Andrews for instructions. According to Billy Murray, of Hot Springs, Arkansas, Bill Dance at that time knew only the rudiments of bass fishing. Billy Murray and I were in his pickup truck pulling a bass boat to fish in Mexico. "Not only did Glenn Andrews show Dance how to find fish," Murray said that hot Texas day in 1971, "but he also showed Bobby and me the ropes. We didn't miss an opportunity to pick Andrews' brains. He was the best. The very best." The Murray twins are well known throughout the world of bassdom. Bobby Murray is the better celebrated as a tournament winner while Billy elected to work with his associate, Jerry McKinnis, filming and producing the "Fishin' Hole" TV series.

A few years ago there was enough bad news to last bass tournament fishing a lifetime. It became known that in Texas a handful of high-stakes anglers connived to cheat by importing fish to the tournament site. The weight of these out-of-state fish brought in and planted, or "staked out" on stringers underwater, was enough to win the attractive purses. These were shared by the men involved in the scheme. The oppressing weight of the outbreaking publicity also was more than one of the men could stand, and he reportedly committed suicide.

Cheating or shaving the rules in tournaments is not a new invention. At the outset of bass for cash contests, rules were loose enough to invite the rare outlaw to exercise his dubious skills in all sorts of profitable ways. To the everlasting credit of Southern Illinois, its tournaments, and those who fished in them, not a hint of scandal has ever surfaced in this region. Some other states could not make this boast.

In the late 1960s through the early 70s it was common practice for those who could afford it to hire professional guides and use their special services just prior to and even during tournament fishing days. Some contestants went a step further and paid guides to "sit" like obedient bird dogs on some of the best fishing holes. Guides would anchor there until the arrival of the contestants who hired them. This widespread, accepted, practice throughout southern states helped to shape "success" stories of many early-day tournament anglers. Obviously the man with the heaviest bankroll and willingness to spend it had the best chance to become the winner.

In Southern Illinois we watched from afar the mistakes made by other tournament promoters, and we learned from them before they became our problems. By 1973 or thereabout some of the deepest wrinkles had been pressed out of tournament regulations. Now fishermen could not hire guides or even be in their company on the lake for a week or more prior to the contest dates. Punishment for being found guilty of cheating was not only expulsion from that particular contest but also from ever again being accepted in future tournaments promoted by the club or organization. Everyone knew these unbending rules.

Cheating of any kind is difficult if not impossible to pull off without complete cooperation between boat partners. Tournament anglers sharing one boat are, in effect, adversaries competing against each other. So, we don't have just one burglar, we have two. The second angler who would cooperate in this form of thievery, however, would be as rare as lips on a chicken. Most tournament fishermen, at the mere hint of using planted fish, would pointedly suggest to stick those bass where the sun doesn't shine. Spines pointed inward, if you will.

An entirely different matter is someone who charitably gives his boat partner fish to weigh in. For example, in the typical singles tournament each person competes as an individual against the field. There are no team scores to consider. As this tournament nears its end it is glaringly evident that one man in the boat has fish though not enough to matter in the final standings. Conversely, the person with whom he is boated might be a contender, and a couple more fish might nail down a placement. Through benevolence alone the also-ran offers his fish. With avarice aforethought they are quickly accepted.

All of these things, and perhaps more, did occasionally occur during the early years of tournaments. Today, regulations coupled with strict supervision are reasons why the cheating scheme in Texas made national news. Generally, there has been so little in bad taste which occurs in bass tournaments that the Texas incident was unusually sensational. For the most part, these contests are colorless, unspectacular events. They are not favorite spectator sports. There isn't enough action to thrill onlookers. Generally, there isn't even enough action to enchant contestants. The truth is that not all bass casters in all tournaments catch fish. Many do not. Many consistently do not.

The largemouth black bass is an unpredictable species. There is no telling when or by whom any given quantity will be caught. During a tournament the number of fish caught per man-hour spent is no more or less than that caught at any other time when no tournaments are being staged. In many contests the number of fish caught per man-hour is significantly fewer than during average fishing days. The difference, of course, is that tournament-caught fish are starkly in evidence at the scales for all to see. Some people are fascinated by what they see while others are repelled. Not everyone agrees with fishing for cash.

What we don't see during an entire fishing season are the hundreds or perhaps thousands of fish per week taken from these same lakes by nontournament anglers. As not all these fish are brought to one place at one time, these multitudes do not come under the critical eye of observers. In most contests the minimum permitted length of bass kept for score is 12 inches, though in many cases in recent years, this minimum has been stretched to 13 and even 14 inches. A 14-inch bass in the average environment will weigh 3 pounds and be in its fourth growing year. Nonetheless, the tournament fisherman who catches a bass just a fraction of an inch shy of this length must return it to the water. Would all nontournament anglers do the same? Not on your boat-calloused butt, they wouldn't. They would take that big sucker home!

Many people, however, still view fishing for cash as totally unacceptable. They feel that the sport and natural resource should not be demeaned by a price tag. They are particularly offended by the thought that this resource is being irrevocably depleted and abused by tournament practices.

It has been established, however, through countless research projects throughout the nation that tournaments do not harm fish populations in healthy environments. First, no one can control weather, which traditionally is lousy during tournaments. If your region suffers from a prolonged earth-cracking drought, a guaranteed remedy is to consult your local bass club and have them whip together a fast tournament. Secondly, man does not have an influence on fish activity. Contest anglers are also bound by the aforementioned rules and size limits of bass, which minimize the taking of immature fish. Finally, the tournament angler is fully aware, perhaps more fully aware than others, that one cannot have bass and eat it too. Whether or not these people are in heated competition on a lake, they keep very few or no bass for themselves.

A commonly heard gripe about tournaments is that they dominate lakes with a glut of high-powered boats filled with arrogant people who have total disregard for the preciously limited space occupied by weekend anglers. Part of this accusation is justified. Bass tournaments do consume much available space on many lakes, and the boat drivers don't waste time while dashing hither and yon seeking out productive fishing holes. Deliberate rudeness, however, is not in the makeup of the average participant. Most tournament rules clearly stipulate that a contestant cannot approach within 50 yards of another boat—any boat. Though I have known a couple renegades who ignored this regulation, they are the rare exceptions. When 100 or more people come together to participate in any activity, be it fishing or a flower show, there will be one or two who attempt to press every possible advantage.

On balance, fishing clubs and the tournaments they promote have been beneficial, not only to the national economy but for everyone who enjoys fishing for any species. Soon after the beginnings of clubs and contests there was an enormous increase in demand for new fishing tackle, boats, motors, and all attendant gear including tourism facilities. That tidal wave swelled in the 1970s, gained momentum during the early '80s, and has not abated since.

General knowledge of the black bass species became widespread only with the advent of fishing clubs and contests. For example, I recall when many fishermen actually believed that in winter fish buried themselves in mud like turtles. Even in Southern Illinois, which abounded with dedicated bassing people, it was common for many to stop all fishing following the spring spawning season. The reason? When bass left shallow water they also left anglers stranded on shorelines, without a notion where bass spent summers. Today the inquisitive novice and veteran alike have at hand a truly incredible amount of factual information about this exceptionally popular fish species.

These revelations touch not only bass fishermen. To the contrary, the habitats, behavior, hours of daily activity, and even some lures and baits are as interchangeable among species as OMC parts for your Johnson and Evinrude outboard motors. So, we shall not only give credit where credit is due—to the bass clubs that launched tournaments—we'll also offer a thought to ponder: If you are the impatient sort who does not want to spend the next 10 years learning just the fundamentals of catching fish, consider joining a fishing club. Even better would be a crash course of hands-on experience in a tournament. This could be the best time and money you'll ever spend on fishing. Remember, you don't have to be a gilt-edged expert to win honors in a tournament.

I recall the first tournament staged for its membership by the Southern Illinois Bass Busters. This even took place on Little Grassy Lake. The purpose of the occasion was to find a temporary home for the newly acquired "challenge trophy." This beautiful silver-plated cup was suitable for having engraved on it the names of club members who won it in competition. The cup-holder had to defend it against all challengers in a one-on-one fish-off. The successful defender retained the cup. If not, it was passed on to the victor. This day on Little Grassy Lake the cup would be presented for the first time.

Bill McCabe, of Johnson City, and I shared a boat, and no sooner had we begun to fish when he startled me with an unexpected comment. "I guess you know," he said, "that everyone figures you to win the contest." I turned, amazed, to look at McCabe, hoping to see a joking expression on his face. If it was there, I couldn't find it. "That's right," he said earnestly. "And they figure you'll win with plastic worms." Whether true or not, if McCabe's comments were designed to scare hell out of me, it worked. Suddenly, I was terrified.

This was a period in Southern Illinois bassing history when few anglers had experience using plastic worms. I was one of those unfortunate few. Most fishermen placed little faith in this lure, so they didn't use it at all or at most sparingly. Now, for some unaccountable reason, I was expected not only to win the contest but to do it with plastic worms. It didn't make sense—except that gradually many of my companions indeed were coming to view this lure with the increased respect it deserved. But I doubted that in my hands the plastic worm that day on Little Grassy deserved *this* much respect.

The fact is that I did win that first challenge trophy tournament. And I did use plastic worms. But not throughout the contest. Perhaps it is not known, until now, by Bass Buster Club members who participated that day that when Bill McCabe bounced that "expected to win" business off me, that I panicked. Off the line came the plastic worm I had intended to use. This was replaced by an entirely different lure.

With this lure within the next hour or so, I managed to catch enough bass to ease the tension, to produce at least a respectable showing. It wasn't until afternoon that I returned to using plastic worms. This switch was profitable. I caught a handsome, thick-bodied five pounder. Nevertheless, without those fish caught earlier with the other lure, I would not have won this tournament. As another man would say, now you know the rest of the story. What was that other lure? At that time it was very common, introduced in the 1950s though it was not widely used in Southern Illinois. It was an ordinary floating Rapala.

A Crab Orchard Lake based bass-fishing tournament that today is still unique in bass-fishing annals took place in 1966, during July and August, in the so-called "dog days" for fishing. Bill Harkins orchestrated this unprecedented event, which would become national news. The contest, which included only two men, lasted 30 consecutive days, which is still a record length for a tournament. Its purpose was to demonstrate beyond question that the dog days syndrome was a myth, that bass could be caught consistently, daily, even during the hottest weeks. Al Peithman was one of the history-making contestants, and I was the other.

The thought of not only testing lures but also having a contest undoubtedly struck Harkins as at the boat dock Peithman and I demurred over the decision to share or not to share the same boat. The lures we preferred and methods of using each were in opposition. Peithman hurled Bombers with a blinding burst of speed, while I employed slow, meticulous efforts in covering the bottom with plastic worms. Finally, we decided on using separate boats, which triggered the tournament question by Harkins.

At the outset, the contest did not pit two men against each other to determine who would catch the heaviest total of bass. To the contrary, it would be a demonstration of lures and opposing fishing methods. More importantly, it would also conclusively prove that bass were eagerly waiting to be caught at a time of summer when fishermen believed otherwise. Harkins would be the official scorekeeper, timer, rules maker, everything of which Peithman and I wanted no part. We would fish daily from separate boats, arrive at the dock each morning at the same time, and come off the lake at an agreed time each day. Harkins would count and record our catches, posting the results on a large board for all to see.

This contest started on July 15, and it would run through August 15. The running account appeared at least every three days in my columns for the *Southern Illinoisan* newspaper, so the event was not wrapped in secrecy. It was the longest, weariest 30 days I've ever used up in any fashion. By the third week both Peithman and I were exhausted physically and mentally. Up each day before sunrise and meeting at the dock, spending a minimum of eight hours daily on the lake under a characteristically scorching sun exacted its expected toll.

We had thought we were armor-plated gladiators of the casting-rod set who would never tire of fishing. That was a myth.

By all accepted standards Peithman won this contest by catching a heavier total weight of accumulated bass, plus the largest bass, during the 30 days. This fish topped six pounds. I caught a slightly greater number of obviously smaller fish. Harkins marked more than 200 bass on his record board, an average of more than six bass per day between the two boats. There were no fishless days between us. It is significant that even on the most productive days our combined catches did not reach the daily limit of 20 fish, or 10 fish each, allowed at that time. Our best day showed 17 bass between us, and, though I caught the lion's share of these, Peithman's fewer bass outweighed mine. So he beat me there, too.

Glenn Andrews, whom you met earlier in this treatise, also figured in this unique contest, though from a great distance. Fliptail plastic worms were only then coming into wide use throughout the South, and Andrews was a distributor of these lures. Though I would not meet Andrews for many months, I got in touch with him and purchased 200 Fliptails, all purple, and slip sinkers and hooks to use with the "Texas rig." He would send them by mail.

When Andrews learned of my mission for these lures, he didn't hesitate to make a prediction of the tournament's outcome. "You will catch more bass with plastic worms," he said flatly, unequivocally, "but the other guy with the Bombers will catch larger fish, and if weight is a factor he'll win the contest." And that's exactly the way it turned out. But I did win the consolation award when *Sports Afield* magazine purchased my story about this event—which article increased interest in summer bass fishing.

Where there are fishing tournaments, there are clubs that sponsor and promote them whether they are for the membership only or open to the public. Many clubs also fund projects of benefit to everyone and the environment. In Southern Illinois various fishing clubs have helped to fund research projects to raise and stock bass and forage fish that game species feed on. They have also purchased and planted trees on shorelines to fight erosion, and it's common for fishing club members to turn out en masse to participate in "clean-up days." They cruise the shorelines and pick up unsightly litter left by the unthinking public.

Then the club members relax. Their club meetings generally are fun events, especially when there is a guest speaker attending and there are special awards to be presented. One annual banquet held by the Crab Orchard Lake Bass Club is a case in point.

It seems that Dick Baker, of Marion, usually arrives late to club functions of all kinds. He even showed up late for this annual banquet at Herrin. "In view of his relaxed schedule," the club secretary, Ron Hudson, announced to the large gathering, "we are giving Baker something to make sure he is never late again." Hudson then removed the wrapping from a cage containing a live rooster.

For engineering the impossible, Sam Davis, of Johnston City, was given an award for being unique. Davis is the only person known to have sunk a fishing boat in the basement of a house. The boat was stored in the basement when torrential rains came and the Davis family was out of town. As flood waters poured in, the boat gradually floated to the ceiling where it could go no farther. But the rising water did, until the boat filled and sank. Davis, by the way, is a plumber.

Club member Carlos Morris, of Marion, was recognized as the outstanding fisherman of the year. Additionally, the club secretary, Hudson, singled him out as the only member who could not swim a stroke. Morris somehow manages to fall in and out of boats safely with shocking regularity, Hudson noted. Morris was presented a length of two-inch-diameter rope with a body harness. "This is to relieve his boat partner of the responsibility of keeping Morris out of the lake," Hudson said, "so that his partner, too, can draw some contentment from fishing."

Guest speaker at this banquet was David Kenney, now former director of the Illinois Department of Conservation. Someone forgot to teach the rooster respect for protocol; its incessant crowing ruptured the harmony of Kenney's speech before the arrogant bird was hustled out the door. Kenney suggested dryly that the rooster should become part of the next banquet dinner.

Sponsoring youth activities is also a part of club activities, such as the aforementioned fund-raising benefit for the Boy Scouts. Generally, area clubs take part in the annual Fishing and Hunting Day celebrations recognized across the nation. This event is designed to inform the public about these outdoor activities. So, the club fishermen you see on lakes are not always only there trying to catch bass. Behind the scenes a lot more takes place within the average club. A great deal of what takes place is of overall advantage to the general public, which is not and perhaps never will be enrolled on a club roster. Not rooster. That one became part of the basic meal during the next annual banquet.

On September 18, 1972, a group of Southern Illinois women officially became the Lunker Ladies Bass Fishing Club. This was the first all-woman fishing organization in this area to announce its intent to engage in bass competitions. The Lunker Ladies club was also one of the first in the nation to become affiliated with a Texas-based group called Bass'n Gals. Spearheaded by a woman called Sugar Farris, Bass'n Gals would become the female answer to the male-dominated national fishing organizations. And Sharon Baker, of Herrin, would become the Lunker Ladies' contribution to Bass'n Gals fishing tournaments staged all over the South.

Women's fishing clubs were inevitable. Regionally, there were more than enough women to support these budding organizations. Nationally the Bass'n Gals flourished in part because of state and regional clubs such as Lunker Ladies. For the first time women who wished to compete in fishing tournaments were not faced with the hassle of bucking the male-oriented system. This system did not originally provide for female participation. Without spelling it out in print within regulations it was, nonetheless, widely accepted that only men would take part in tournaments sponsored by all-male clubs whether regional, state, or national organizations.

For a woman to take part in these events was unheard of, and when it was rumored that one would, the arguments pro and con rose to fever pitch. Some men threatened to pull out of these contests if women participated, while others cheered on the prospect of lifting the unspoken ban on women tournament casters. Organizations such as Lunker Ladies and Bass'n Gals solved the problem. Many of the women in these proved beyond doubt that they were equal to or even better than their male counterparts with artificial lure manipulation for big-money prizes.

Sharon Baker served her apprenticeship on the tournament circuit of Bass'n Gals without experiencing overwhelming success. Competing against the best in the nation in these contests, Baker did not initially come away showered with glory. To climb the ladder of success was painstakingly slow. Baker had to learn through observation and trial and error what many of those whom she competed against already knew. Many of the Bass'n Gals anglers were wives of professional guides and men already celebrated for their own tournament accomplishments. These women were not classed as your basic novice anglers. To the contrary, they were ready-made professionals looking for the time and place to assert their professionalism. The Bass'n Gals competitions provided that.

Nonetheless, each time Baker competed she raised the finishing stats a notch or two, until she persistently pulled away from the also-rans, finally becoming a major contender in each contest she entered. In recent years she has placed highly, among the top 20, or consistently higher than most women who compete regularly, and she is the only one from Southern Illinois who has etched such a deep mark on the slate of bass-fishing contests of national significance. We can say, too, that Baker's dedication to competitive fishing overshadows any accomplishment by a male resident angler of Southern Illinois who has competed on the same level. Although a number of men have occasionally fished the big-money national events, none have punched a dent in the records as Baker has managed to do in her league.

The future for women's tournaments looks especially bright as its scope expands to include lakes in the Upper Midwest as well as in the South and Southwest. While the cash prizes in all-female competitions haven't exactly rocketed to the heights of the cash prizes in male events, they have more recently approached nearly those altitudes.

Trophies and Taxidermy

Just a few easy steps will prepare your trophy fish for its visitation to the taxidermist. Obviously, from the moment you make the decision to have the fish mounted, you'll want to give it the respect due a team of stern-faced IRS agents investigating your accounts. First, carefully fold down to their natural posture the fish's dorsal and other fins. Now, wrap the fish in a wet cloth or newspapers, being especially mindful of the above appendages. Also maintain the fish's natural stretched-out length. Do not fold or bend.

If the fish is to be delivered to the taxidermist the same day it is caught, there is no need to freeze it, though keeping it on ice is a prudent measure to take. On the other hand if it will be a day or a few before this trip is made, freezing is a good choice, if this can be done without bending the fish to fit the compartment. Chances are that when he receives the fish the taxidermist will freeze it anyway. Few of these professionals have time to get at newly acquired specimens the day they are brought in.

It has been this writer's experience that it is far better to seek the services of local and regional taxidermists than to send fish off to who knows where. Given the same professionalism, the same skillful handling of the transaction, and the same result hanging on the wall, it is to everyone's advantage to have it done locally. There is something about Jiffy 24-hour Taxidermy Services which doesn't instill in me the greatest confidence. I get the disquieting feeling that the fish I sent airmail is being passed somewhere over Tulsa by the one I'm going to receive. It is more comforting to deal with someone we can see, talk to, and perhaps get just a little cranky with when six months pass and the fish is still in his freezer. It took nature less time to form the fields of coal beneath Southern Illinois than it takes for the average taxidermist to complete a fish. But, it's your fish.

Although a particular fish, a largemouth bass, was not my personal property, it was in my trust to be taken to a taxidermist for Bill Bickers, a friend from Champaign. Bickers caught this bass, his first six pounder, from Little Grassy Lake. He wanted the fish mounted, and rightly so, but his schedule didn't permit a layover in Carbondale. I would keep the bass for him, freeze it, and when convenient would take it to Jack Etherton, a Jonesboro taxidermist. There was nothing wrong with the plan. It was the execution of it which went awry.

The trophy bass had been carefully wrapped atop the freezer in our garage when my wife, Melba, announced a phone call for me. I left the fish and answered the phone. I also left the fish where it rested the remainder of that day, all night, and the following day. Completely forgot about it. Until the third day. The temperature didn't help any. It was about 85 degrees and soaring. My wife's sensitive nose alerted her to the fact that something in the garage was decaying. She investigated the package containing the ripened bass. She also, then, recalled the agreement I had with Bill Bickers, so as quickly as possible, while suffering the stink, she put the bass in the freezer.

Later that day, Melba would tell me that the bass had not been in the freezer more than a half hour when Zeke "Hollywood" Davidson, of Anna, dropped by the house. Finding me not home he stayed only a minute, she said, but that was time enough for what she had in mind. She asked him if he would drop the fish off at Etherton's on his way back to Anna. Davidson readily agreed to take it with him and drop it by Etherton's, since Jonesboro is next door to Anna. Seeing Melba take the package from the freezer and even carry it to his car, Davidson naturally assumed the fish was frozen solid.

On the way back to Anna, Davidson made a number of stops, and each time he got back in his car the fragrance of the fish was immensely more powerful. He would admit later that the stupefying smell literally drove him from Carbondale dashing wildly with all windows wide open down Route 51 toward Anna-Jonesboro. "That was the slowest 20 miles I've ever driven that fast," Davidson said. "And if it hadn't been for the air conditioner belting me right in the face, I don't think I would have made it."

Bickers' trophy bass was none the worse for the experience. Taking it in stride, Etherton put the fish in his freezer to calm down, become harmless. About six months was plenty of time. During his first visit the following spring, Bickers collected his trophy mount. It was a beautiful specimen. He was so pleased with it that I never did tell him any of the sordid details preceding his fish's reaching the wall plaque stage.

The moral to this story is that it's better to ignore phone calls while wrapping fish for the freezer in the garage on a hot day. If you must take attention-diverting calls be sure to bear in mind that Zeke Davidson felt compelled to trade his relatively new car within days following that mad flight down the highway to Jonesboro. I never did ask Zeke why he wanted to trade off a perfectly good car. Perhaps the air conditioner was inadequate.

Art Reid has been since 1971 the producer/host of the nationally acclaimed syndicated television series "Outdoors with Art Reid," produced by WSIU-TV (Southern Illinois University, Carbondale). From 1954 to 1965 and from 1965 to 1980, respectively, he was the outdoors editor for the *News-Gazette* (Champaign-Urbana, Illinois) and the *Southern Illinoisan* (Carbondale). He has also been a syndicated newspaper columnist, the midwestern field editor of *Shooting Times*, the freshwater fishing editor of *American Angler*, and has published over 300 feature articles in various nationally known outdoors magazines including *Field & Stream* and *Sports Afield*. During more than 30 years of fishing statewide, Reid has caught all species of sport fish found in Illinois with the sole exception of muskellunge. In recent years the author and his wife, Melba, have traveled and fished across the nation, writing about and filming their experiences for articles and television shows. Reid's travels have taken him all over North and Central America as well as to Australia. The author's work has been honored by the Arkansas Wildlife Association, the Friends of Morris Library (Southern Illinois University, Carbondale), the American Association for Conservation Information, and the Izaak Walton League of America.